D0368024

YOUNG SURVIVORS
OF THE HOLOCAUST

By Allan Zullo

SCHOLASTIC INC.

To my good friends Jeffrey and Barbara Wasserman, whose commitment to Jewish culture is matched only by their love of life.
— A.Z.

ISBN 978-0-545-90975-4

10 9 8 7 6 5 4 3 2 1   16 17 18 19 20

Printed in the U.S.A.   40
First printing 2016

Book design by Cheung Tai

ACKNOWLEDGMENTS

I wish to extend my heartfelt gratitude to the Holocaust survivors featured in this book for their willingness to relive, in personal interviews with me, their painful and emotional memories of the horrors they experienced as children.

Special thanks go to the following for their much-appreciated cooperation and guidance: Emily Potter, program assistant, Office of Survivor Affairs of the United States Holocaust Memorial Museum (ushmm.org), who was instrumental in putting me in touch with several child survivors; Paul Orbuch, founding president and chairman emeritus of the Jewish Partisan Educational Foundation (jewishpartisans .org) for his cooperation and support; and Sheri Pearl, JPEF's director of development, who supplied me with valuable contact information.

I also want to thank Lesley Weiss; Wayne Friedman; and Maureen Carter, Holocaust studies program planner for the School District of Palm Beach County, Florida.

AUTHOR'S NOTE

❧

You are about to read ten incredible true stories of brave boys and girls who survived the Holocaust. These accounts are based exclusively on the personal, lengthy interviews that I conducted with each person featured in this book. Using real names, dates, and places, the stories are written as factual and truthful versions of the survivors' recollections. Because of their young ages during the Holocaust, their memories, in some cases, were formed by what their parents or older siblings told them happened.

If you see an asterisk after a name, it means the person was real but the name is not, because the survivor couldn't remember it or didn't know it. Also, the dialogue has been re-created for dramatic effect. The words *Nazis* and *Germans* are used interchangeably, but, for the purposes of this book, the word *Germans* refers to troops and not necessarily the German people. To help you understand various German words and Holocaust-related terms, please use the glossary in the back of this book.

Much of what you will read in the following pages is disturbing and horrifying because that's the way it really happened. It's hard to imagine that anyone, especially children, could bear so much suffering from so much cruelty.

But this book is also a celebration of the human spirit—of the will to overcome unspeakable horrors, the will to triumph over evil, the will to live. Each person's experience reveals that in the most horrible and hopeless situations, young people can rely on their courage, faith, and smarts—and sometimes sheer luck—to escape from almost certain death.

Not only did these brave Jewish children survive the Holocaust, but they grew up, got married, and have enjoyed happy, productive lives. All of them have also turned their harrowing experiences into lessons for future generations by speaking at schools, churches, synagogues, conferences, and other gatherings.

I hope you find the accounts in this book extraordinary and inspiring, and that you understand how important it is to keep recalling the past . . . so no one ever forgets.

—Allan Zullo

CONTENTS

CONTENTS

THE HOLOCAUST

L ed by dictator Adolf Hitler, the Nazi Party in Germany in the 1930s and 1940s believed that certain people—especially Jews, Gypsies, gays, lesbians, and the disabled—were inferior and didn't deserve to live.

The Nazis were anti-Semitic, which means they hated the Jewish people. Although many Jews were doctors, lawyers, businessmen, bankers, and teachers who contributed much to German society, Hitler blamed them for the country's economic problems. In truth, Germany was going through a difficult time because it had been badly defeated in World War I, which ended in 1918.

Hitler had two major goals: invade and occupy all of Europe and exterminate the Jews.

In March 1938, Germany annexed Austria, which a majority of non-Jewish Austrians welcomed. Then, in September 1939, Germany invaded Poland. Because of a secret prewar agreement, Germany occupied the western half of the country while the Soviet Union (including Russia) controlled the eastern half.

Great Britain and France, who were allies of Poland, declared war on Germany, triggering World War II. The following year, Nazi forces controlled all of Poland, and invaded and occupied Denmark, Norway, Belgium, Holland, and Luxembourg. Then France fell, and Great Britain was battered by German air assaults. Next, Germany launched a surprise attack against Russia in June 1941 and occupied such Soviet countries as Lithuania and the Ukraine. In December 1941, the United States entered the war and teamed up with several countries, including Great Britain and the Free French (the resistance forces fighting for the liberation of France). They formed the Allied forces and waged a fierce campaign to dismantle the German war machine.

Hitler was determined to protect at all costs "German blood and German honor" for the country's Aryans, the name given to white, non-Jewish Germans. As country after country fell under German occupation, Jews were singled out for brutal mistreatment. Hitler and his parliament passed laws stripping Jews of their rights, jobs, homes, and businesses. Jews had to wear the six-pointed Star of David, a symbol of Judaism, on their sleeves, chests, or backs to tell them apart from gentiles (non-Jews). They couldn't walk freely in the streets or do many of the things Europeans took for granted. Signs in theaters, cafés, restaurants, and other public places warned that Jews weren't allowed to enter. To enforce these laws, the police organization known as the Gestapo and an elite army corps known as the Waffen-SS—along with anti-Semitic local police, paramilitary groups, and foreign soldiers—beat, tortured, and murdered Jews.

During the war years, the Nazis created ghettos. These were small areas inside cities that were sealed by brick or stone walls or barbed wire where Jews were forced to live under unhealthy and overcrowded conditions. Every month, hundreds of thousands of Jews were deported—shipped in crammed cattle cars to inhumanely run concentration camps. Unless Jews were useful to the Nazis as slave laborers, they were killed in gas chambers or murdered in other ways. Meanwhile, in countless massacres outside of ghettos and villages, Nazi henchmen were machine-gunning Jews, who tumbled into mass graves that, in many cases, they had been ordered to dig.

It was all part of Hitler's "Final Solution"—the depraved Nazi plan to exterminate all the Jews of Europe.

Why would such cruelty go virtually unchecked? Out of fear, anti-Semitism, or self-protection, millions of non-Jewish Europeans couldn't or wouldn't get involved in stopping the Nazi madness. It's estimated that only one half of one percent of them have been declared Righteous Gentiles—non-Jews who risked their lives to assist and hide Jews. Sadly, many Europeans actively supported the Nazis by turning in Jews and those who assisted Jews. These morally bankrupt Nazi sympathizers were known as collaborators or informants.

Most of the victims shipped to death camps had been tricked into believing they were being sent to decent work camps. Most Jews couldn't conceive that Germany—a civilized country that introduced the world to the beautiful music of Bach, Beethoven, and Brahms—was capable of murdering a whole race of people. As a result, the unknowing Jews didn't revolt at first. Most had no choice about whether or not to fight, anyway, because they never had the chance to take up arms.

But from the beginning, they rebelled in subtle ways. Jews smuggled thousands of their children to safety, sneaked food and medicine into ghettos, forged documents so they could pass as gentiles, and sabotaged weapons and other items that they, as slave laborers, were forced to make for the Germans. In defiance of Nazi laws, Jews in the ghettos and concentration camps held prayer services, taught children to read Hebrew, wrote poems and songs, and painted pictures to maintain their dignity, self-respect, and faith.

As the truth about mass exterminations slowly leaked out, thousands of Jews fought back. Some of them escaped from concentration camps and ghettos to form or join guerilla warfare groups known as partisans. Others worked with secret organizations of gentiles for the underground, or the resistance movement. These fighters for freedom excelled in disrupting Nazi supply lines. They blew up trains, destroyed vital bridges, blocked major roads, and cut communication lines. They also sabotaged numerous enemy power plants and factories and triggered uprisings in ghettos and prison camps.

As the war came to an end in 1945, the Allies liberated imprisoned and hidden Jews, although hundreds of thousands were barely alive because of Nazi savagery. The world was shocked to discover that of the nine million Jews who lived in Europe before the war, six million (including three million Polish Jews) had been murdered or died from starvation or disease in Nazi camps. Of the Jewish children who failed to escape Europe after 1939, more than 1.5 million were murdered by the Nazis or were deported to camps, where they died of illness or hunger. Another five million non-Jewish civilians died at the hands of the Nazis.

The name Holocaust is derived from an ancient Greek word meaning "sacrifice by fire." Over time, the word has come to mean the horrific slaughter of human beings on a massive scale.

Out of the ashes of the Holocaust emerged Israel—the rebirth of the Jewish homeland—where in 1948 hundreds of thousands of Jews started a new life they hoped would be free from the tyranny of hate. Many Holocaust survivors chose to remain in Europe, while others came to the United States or settled in other countries. The survivors all had one hope: to put together the pieces of their shattered lives. They each had a story to tell. Now, with each passing year, the number of Holocaust survivors dwindles as they pass on from old age.

Their stories deserve to be told because only by learning from these cautionary tales can we help make a better world.

NO WAY OUT

CHUNA GRYNBAUM

(Henry Greenbaum)

Sixteen-year-old Chuna Grynbaum was excited—and terrified. He and his older sister Faiga were set to escape the slave labor camp near Starachowice, Poland, that for years had been a living nightmare for them and thousands of other Jews.

In the dark of night, several prisoners had already sneaked through holes cut in a barbed wire fence and an outer wooden fence. Now it was nearing Chuna and Faiga's turn. Just as they were ready to rush the holes, a guard dog barked and the searchlights from the watchtowers turned on. Sweeping back and forth, the lights zeroed in on escapees who were slipping through the fences.

"Halt! Halt!" the guards shouted. Whistles blew, alarms blared, and the camp exploded in gunfire. Searchlights pivoted left and right, revealing men and women running in all directions. Some kept trying to crawl their way to freedom while others dived into the darkness.

Still holding Faiga's hand, Chuna began running for his life. In the bright beams, he saw prisoners gunned down in mid-stride. Trying to dodge the searchlights, he heard bullets whizzing past him at frighteningly close range. Suddenly, a beam caught him for just a second or two. But that's all it took for a guard to see Chuna and shoot. The bullet struck Chuna on the right side of the back of his head.

He felt himself falling. Then everything turned to black.

Chuna was the youngest in a large family—six sisters and two brothers—in Starachowice (pronounced star-a-hoe-VIT-za), home of a large military-industrial complex that included ironworks and factories that produced artillery and ammunition. While his mother, Gittel, raised the family, his father, Nochem, an Orthodox Jew, ran a tailor shop out of their home and was also caretaker of the neighborhood synagogue four doors down.

Life was good for a boy like Chuna. But in 1939, when he was 11, he sensed his parents' unease over the anti-Semitic rantings of Hitler that were broadcast over the radio. And then there were the rumors of an impending invasion. Some of Chuna's siblings wanted the family to emigrate to America, where Diana, their married sister who had left in 1937, was living. But his parents felt it was better to stay put because Poland was all they knew.

As anti-Semitism intensified, Nochem heard that Jews who worked in one of the arms factories would be treated better than others if the Germans invaded. Through a friend, a Catholic who was a manager of a munitions plant, Nochem landed jobs for his son Chuna and daughters Ita, 13, Chaja, 19, and Faiga, 30. Faiga's husband had emigrated to the United States, but he hadn't been able to get her and their 7-year-old daughter, Pola, out of the country yet.

Life started to unravel for the Grynbaum family that summer. Tragedy struck in June when Nochem died unexpectedly, leaving Chuna's older brother David, a 26-year-old master tailor, as the family's main breadwinner. Then, ten weeks later, on September 1, 1939, Germany invaded Poland, triggering World War II.

Fleeing the bombing, Chuna, David, Gittel, Chaja, Ita, Faiga, and Pola sought safety on the farm of a family friend. (Chuna's married sisters Rozia and Brondel went elsewhere with their children; his other brother, Zachary, was serving in the Polish Army.) On the Grynbaums' third day on the farm, German troops were advancing nearby. Fearing they would kill him, David fled.

The remaining members of the family returned to Starachowice and began life under the Germans, who established anti-Semitic laws and took over the armament factories where Chuna and his sisters worked eight-hour shifts for little money. The plant melted down scrap metal to make ammunition and parts for vehicles. Chuna, now 12, operated a machine that made heavy-duty springs for trucks and tanks.

In October 1940, the Germans created a barbed wire ghetto, cramming thousands of Jews into a small three-block area of Starachowice. Chuna's family, including his married sisters Brondel and Rozia and their six children, lived together with various relatives in a jam-packed apartment.

A year later, around 4:00 a.m. on the morning of October 27, 1941, Chuna and his family were jolted awake by loud pounding on the apartment door. A Nazi officer gruffly announced, "Every man, woman, and child must show up at the marketplace by 9:00 a.m. Bring only what you can carry. Anyone who remains behind for any reason will be shot on the spot."

Not knowing what evil the Germans had in store for them, the Grynbaums arrived at a sprawling field where farmers had come weekly to sell their produce. On this day, there were no farmers, just Nazis and Ukrainian and Lithuanian guards. The only product offered at this marketplace was terror for the more than 5,000 Jews who showed up. This was the start of a *Selektion*, (German for "selection") when family members were ripped apart from one another—chosen individually by an officer's finger to go either here or there.

The air was filled with moans, cries, and shrieks as children were separated from mothers, husbands from wives, grandparents and the disabled from caregivers. Whips were cracked and guns were fired at those who refused to let go of each other. In the distance, more shots rang out, chilling sounds that meant someone had just paid the ultimate price for not appearing at the marketplace. Walking nervously up to an officer were Chuna, his mother, five sisters, and their six children. Chuna handed over the identification papers showing that he, Ita, Chaja, and Faiga worked in the factory.

Seeing Faiga holding the hand of her young daughter, the officer asked Faiga, "Do you still want to work?" When she nodded, he motioned for her daughter to stand next to Gittel. Then the officer ordered Gittel, Brondel, Rozia, and the children to move to one section of the field and motioned Chuna and his three other sisters to the other side. There would be no work for an older woman—Gittel was 54—and mothers with small children.

As soldiers shoved Gittel away, Chuna protested, "Where are you taking them?"

Gittel tried to break free to give Chuna a hug good-bye, but the guards pushed her back with the butts of their guns. Tears welling up in his eyes, Chuna stood helplessly watching his mother get swallowed up in the crowd. "Take care of your little brother!" she shouted to Faiga, Chaja, and Ita. Then his mother disappeared along with his two other sisters and his six nieces and nephews.

This can't be happening, Chuna told himself. *It's not fair. It's not right.* He closed his eyes, hoping he could recapture the image of his mother's face. *This is the worst moment of my life.* He didn't know his heart could hurt so much.

By early afternoon, the elderly, the young, the physically and mentally challenged, mothers clutching babies, and anyone else deemed unfit to work were pushed into boxcars amid wailing and gunshots. As the transport of human cargo pulled away, Chuna, his three sisters, and 2,000 other Jews were ordered to form a massive column—five to a row, 400 rows. Then they were forced to jog, not walk, away from the city for about three and a half miles (five and a half kilometers). Snarling dogs and trigger-happy guards forced them to keep moving. Those who fell were whipped, and if they didn't get up, they were shot where they lay.

Chuna and the others were herded to the top of a stone quarry where the Nazis had built a slave labor camp known as Julag 1. It was surrounded by a six-foot-high wooden outer fence and a tall inner fence made of barbed wire. By the time they reached the camp, those who had been carrying bags or suitcases had dropped them along the way.

At the entrance, an officer told them, "If you want to live, empty all your pockets and dump your jewelry into the box next to me. If we find anything of value on you, you will be shot."

I have nothing, thought Chuna, *not even a mother or father.*

Men and women were assigned separate barracks. Like each prisoner, Chuna was given a thin blanket. The bunks were nothing but six-foot-wide shelves with no mattresses or straw. Using their blankets as pillows, the men slept in their clothes, three to a bunk. There wasn't enough room for Chuna to sleep on his back because he and his bunk mates were squeezed in so tightly. When one turned over, they all turned over. Night after night, the 13-year-old boy cried himself to sleep while pining for his mother.

But even though his sisters were in a different barrack from his, Chuna often saw them, especially Faiga, who took on the role of his mother. While his sisters toiled as seamstresses, he worked in a plant that made antiaircraft shells.

Julag 1 grew to hold as many as 5,000 prisoners at one time. Like the other Jews, Chuna was given a slice of bread and a cup of what passed for coffee at breakfast and cabbage soup (which had no cabbage) at dinner. Cruelty was on the daily menu.

As part of his job, Chuna and another boy, Patryk*, took the shells that had been formed in a furnace and brought them outside to cool in the sand. One day, the two accidentally let one slip through their hands. When it fell, it knocked over an entire row of cooling shells like dominoes. Nothing was broken or damaged and the boys quickly stood the shells back up.

When they returned to the camp, Chuna and Patryk were singled out for punishment. They were taken by guards and put in two separate rooms that each had a chair bolted to the floor. Chuna was ordered to take off his shirt and made to kneel in front of the chair, place his chest on the seat, and put his head through an opening in the chair back. Then a guard brought out a whip and lashed him. Chuna cried out in pain with every crack of the whip on his bare back. Through the wall, he could hear Patryk yelling in agony, too.

"The more you scream, the more I hit you," the guard snarled.

The whip snapped again and again until Chuna was numb. When the lashing was over, the guard refused to let Chuna put on his shirt or use any medication on the wounds. Chuna didn't sleep that night or the next three nights because he couldn't lie on his back or side without excruciating pain. He rested by sitting on the barrack floor. The same held true for Patryk.

The months of a hungry, torturous existence dragged on for one year, then two. Every night, Chuna thought of his mother, which always brought tears. He used his imagination to conjure up the sweet aroma that wafted throughout the house when his mama baked those mouthwatering cookies. And he pretended to hear her lovely voice sing a folk song about raisins and nuts when she tucked him in at bedtime. He also whispered a prayer—a short, simple one: "Dear Lord, please help me survive so I can one day see my sister Diana in America."

Chuna and his fellow slaves never washed with soap because they had none. To get clean, they sometimes covered themselves in mud and then rinsed it off with cold water from a well's hand pump. They were never given a haircut or a chance to clean their clothes. As a result, their hair and clothes became a haven for lice, leading to an epidemic of highly contagious typhus. Most everyone, including Chuna and Faiga, contracted typhus, which causes high fever, flu-like symptoms, and rashes. Left untreated, it can lead to death, especially for those who are already in poor physical condition and lack proper nutrition.

Fortunately for Chuna and Faiga, they had low fevers, so they still went to work even though they felt dizzy. He knew what happened to those who were too sick to work. They were taken away and never seen again.

In 1943, Chuna's sister Ita contracted typhus, which left her so weak and feverish that she simply couldn't get out of her bunk. With no medicine, her condition worsened. Chuna visited her after his factory shift, sitting down beside her and crying with her. Seeing her covered in bedsores because she had no mattress or straw to lie on, he smuggled a handful of clean rags from the factory so she could rest on something softer than a wood plank.

A week later, when he went to see Ita after his night shift, he couldn't find her. He asked Jakob*, a Jewish inmate who had been a policeman, "Do you know what happened to my sister Ita?"

"Yes," Jakob replied, his eyes downcast. "She died during the night, so we buried her in the bottom of the stone quarry. I'm sorry, Chuna." Ita was 17.

While Chuna was reeling from Ita's death, his sister Chaja, 23, also contracted typhus and became too sick to work. Within days, she was taken away with several extremely ill prisoners. She and the others never returned.

Overwhelmed with grief, the boy with the once large family now had only one sibling left who could console him, his 34-year-old sister Faiga. She was Chuna's rock, the strong one, the substitute mother who comforted and encouraged him. At least he still had her. He also had, in the camp, an older cousin whose name was Ita, the same as one of his deceased sisters.

Ever since Faiga had arrived at Julag 1, she had been working in the tailor shop, catering to high-ranking officers of the Gestapo and SS. As one of 50 seamstresses, Faiga specialized in repairing and altering uniforms and was given extra bread rations, which she shared with Chuna, helping him survive.

In July 1944, a year after the inmates had been moved to a nearby slave labor camp known as Julag 2, Faiga took Chuna aside and whispered to him, "We're going to escape tomorrow night. An officer came into the tailor shop last week and told us to hurry up with the alterations on the uniforms because the camp was being liquidated in about ten days and that we'll be deported. When we returned to the barrack, we talked it over. If the Nazis are going to ship us out after three years, they're probably going to kill us. They don't need us anymore."

Chuna nodded and said, "Whenever anyone is deported, we never hear about them ever again. We still don't know what happened to Mama and the others."

"Someone smuggled in a pair of clippers from the factory, and we'll use it to cut a hole in the barbed wire fence," Faiga said. "When you return from your factory job tomorrow night, do not go into your barrack. Wait for me outside. It'll be pitch-dark and I'll come get you. Be ready to escape."

"Oh, Faiga, I'm ready. I can't wait to get out of this hell."

That night, all he could think about was fleeing the camp and making his way to America. He was too pumped up to get much sleep. The next day, he could barely concentrate at the factory. When he returned to the camp that night, he anxiously stood in the darkness outside his barrack. The searchlights on the watchtowers were off.

After a few tense minutes, he heard Faiga whisper, "Chuna." She was accompanied by Jakob, the former policeman. "I know where the hole is," Jakob said. "Let's go."

With Faiga holding Jakob's hand and Chuna's, the three of them bent low and scurried toward the first fence, the one made of barbed wire. About 10 feet away, they huddled with a small gathering of inmates. Two other groups were escaping through a three-foot-wide gap in the cut barbed wire fence and a hole they quietly had made in the outer wood fence. "We're next," Faiga whispered to Chuna, squeezing his hand.

But when one of the escapees ahead of them tried to make the hole in the wooden fence bigger, he was too noisy. That's when a guard dog barked, alerting the guards, who turned on the searchlights and began firing at those attempting to escape. It was then that Chuna scrambled for cover and was shot in the head.

After he regained consciousness a few minutes later, he felt dazed and disoriented, and his head was bleeding badly. As his mind began to clear, he realized how close he had come to death. The bullet had grazed his skull, causing a nasty three-inch gash. He staggered to his feet and looked around. Faiga and Jakob were nowhere in sight. "Faiga! Faiga!" he shouted. "Where are you?" *Did she think I was dead? Did she escape? Was she killed? Maybe she went back to her barrack.*

Searchlights were still streaming back and forth, and gunfire continued to echo throughout the camp. Ducking to avoid the lights, Chuna reached Faiga's barrack and opened the door.

A woman gasped when she saw Chuna's bloody head. She started to shove him back out the door, screaming, "Get out! Get out! You'll have us all killed if they find you in here!"

Chuna stood his ground. "All I want to do is find my sister Faiga."

"She's not here."

"How do you know? You haven't even looked."

"Leave here right now!" she ordered, trying again to push him back.

"No, they're still shooting out there."

Just then, a guard in the yard began randomly firing into the barrack. Women jumped off the bunks and dived onto the floor. Chuna did, too. A few bullets tore into the building, but none hit anyone.

After the shooting stopped, Chuna got to his feet and began searching for Faiga in the barrack. He found his cousin Ita, who looked horrified when she saw the blood oozing from his head. After telling him Faiga wasn't there, Ita found a rag, soaked it in a bucket of water, and wiped the blood off his head. Then she used a dry rag as a bandage over the wound. She took off her hat—a beret she had worn since her deportation—and put it on Chuna's head to cover the wound and hold the rag in place to stem the bleeding. "You should get out of here," she told him. "They'll kill you if they catch you in here."

He slipped out and hid in the shadows. *If they spot me, they'll know that I was trying to escape*, he thought. Waiting for the searchlight to pass, he dashed back to his barrack without being discovered. When he returned to his bunk, he thought,

Thank God I'm safe. And then he prayed that Faiga was safe, too.

Shortly before dawn, the prisoners were abruptly awakened and ordered outside for *Appell* (roll call) so the guards could determine who had escaped during the night. Chuna and the others were ordered to face the barracks until the count was completed. During this time, he could hear moaning and crying behind him. His nerves were on edge because he was afraid the guards would notice his wound. Fortunately, the rag and Ita's beret had stopped the bleeding. Throughout *Appell*, Chuna kept thinking about Faiga, hoping she had escaped.

By the time the count was over, dawn had broken over the camp. "Turn around and face the fence!" an officer ordered the inmates. When they did, many winced and gasped. Bodies were sprawled throughout the yard and on both sides of the barbed wire fence. Several prisoners who had tried to escape lay bleeding, groaning, or begging for a doctor. There were pleas: "Kill me." "Shoot me." "Put me out of my misery."

Chuna's eyes scanned the yard for Faiga, fearing he would spot her corpse. She wasn't among the dead. Neither was she among the wounded. *Maybe she escaped.* His spirits rose. Then he noticed a young man slumped against the barbed wire, his breathing labored, his torso covered in blood. *It's Jakob! He's still alive!*

To the inmates at *Appell*, a camp officer ranted about the escape attempt. "No one escapes here!" he bellowed. "Do you know what we do to those who try to escape?" He signaled to the guards. They strode over to each wounded person and shot them dead. When it was Jakob's turn to die, Chuna watched the guard shoot him. Jakob toppled to the ground, revealing the body of a dead woman that had been blocked from Chuna's view and was lying on the other side of the barbed wire fence. Staring at it, Chuna stifled a sob from deep within his soul. *Oh, my God, it's Faiga!*

The raging camp officer continued his outburst, boasting that all those who managed to sneak out had been hunted down and executed. But Chuna heard none of that. His whole being shook with grief over the death of his beloved sister. Suddenly, he felt an emptiness that terrified him. The one person he had counted on to help him survive this dreadful place, the one person who provided comfort and support in all the misery and torment they suffered, was dead. Never again would he feel her motherly touch or swallow the food she shared with him or listen to her soothing words.

Faiga is gone forever, and now I have no one, Chuna told himself. *Dear God, I am 16 years old and all alone. I never did anything bad. I came from a very religious home. Please help me. I leave it in your hands that someday I can make it to America to be with my sister Diana.*

Winding up his tirade, the camp officer sent the inmates off to their regular slave labor jobs and held some prisoners back to repair the fences and remove the bodies.

Days later, the Germans liquidated the camp, using extra Ukrainian guards and dogs to herd inmates into cattle cars. When the prisoners assumed they were bound for a death camp, many attempted to flee. Chuna was already in one of the cars and didn't move. The guards killed 300 immediately and tracked down and murdered others who had reached the forest.

The remaining 1,500 prisoners were stuffed into pitch-dark, nearly airless boxcars. After Chuna's group was sealed up in the car, inmates fought to be near a tiny window to sniff fresh air. Chuna stayed by the strongest men, figuring that if they tried to escape, he would go with them.

For more than two days, they traveled under conditions that couldn't have been more miserable—packed tightly in an unbearably hot, stuffy, foul boxcar. At every stop, they cried out in several different languages for water. The heartless guards wouldn't give them a drop or even a bucket to urinate in.

On the third day, they arrived at the notorious death camp Auschwitz. When the doors opened up, Chuna got a whiff that made him gag. Gray ash fluttered down like snow. The stench and cinders were coming from the crematoriums that were incinerating the bodies of Jews murdered in the gas chambers. As the prisoners stepped out, they faced another *Selektion.* Some were ordered to the left and never seen again; others, like Chuna, were sent to the right.

The Germans then stripped Chuna of all he possessed other than his life. They took away his name and gave him a new identity—the tattoo A18991 on his left arm. Next, his long scraggly hair was cut for the first time in three years.

Chuna and his group were ordered to undress and toss away their clothes, the same that they had been wearing since they arrived at Julag 1 in 1941. Then they were given soap and their first shower in years. Before Chuna washed himself, he stood under the shower, opened his mouth wide, and drank until his terrible thirst was quenched. Once the inmates were clean, they were given striped uniforms and canvas shoes with wooden soles.

Soon he and 49 other inmates were marched about four miles (six kilometers) from Auschwitz to a subcamp called Buna-Monowitz, where slave labor was used in a factory owned by the German company IG Farben, which provided chemicals—including the gas used to kill the Jews and others—for the Nazi war machine.

Chuna, whose head wound had become infected, was put on a crew building a cobblestone road to the factory. His job was to fill his wheelbarrow with gravel, sand, or stone from railcars and transport it to the construction site. Without gloves, his hands became covered with painful blisters. Workers were routinely beaten or whipped. For Chuna, the only good thing about Buna was that the stench from Auschwitz wasn't as strong from this far away.

The inmates received little food and were worked to exhaustion. One day, a starving teenage laborer tried to pick up scraps of food that had been tossed outside the kitchen door by a prisoner who cooked for the German officers. The laborer was caught and hanged the next day.

Chuna dreamed about escaping but knew he had no chance. Besides, the officers warned the inmates that for every person who attempted to escape, five prisoners would be executed. Because of this real threat, inmates kept an eye on one another to prevent anyone from fleeing.

By early 1945, Allied planes began bombing German factories and railroad lines. When the factory in Buna-Monowitz was attacked, the guards and their dogs hid in bunkers but made the *Kapos* and prisoners continue to work.

The factory was severely damaged, so Chuna and other slave laborers were stuffed into cattle cars and sent to a concentration camp in Flossenbürg, Germany, where they bundled clothes that once belonged to Jews before they were exterminated. In the distance, he could hear Allied artillery drawing closer to the camp. Two days before the Allies liberated the camp, Chuna and about 150 of his fellow prisoners were put into open boxcars and transported through Bavaria. But they were forced to abandon the train after planes attacked it.

Just when Chuna thought they would be liberated at any moment, the Germans ordered the inmates to begin a death march toward the Dachau concentration camp. For several weeks in snow and rain, Chuna and his fellow prisoners trudged during the day and slept in the woods at night. When they walked past certain villages, members of the Hitler Youth organization threw rocks at them and spit on them. The prisoners drank out of frozen creeks and chewed rotting leaves to stave off hunger. Occasionally, they stopped at a farmhouse, where the guards ordered the inhabitants to give each prisoner a potato. The sick, weak, and exhausted collapsed and died or were shot to death for failing to keep up with the marchers. By mid-April, half of the group had perished. The surviving prisoners made a pledge to one another: "If you live through this, tell the world what the Nazis have done."

In late April, the marchers were slogging past a farm during a rainstorm when they saw low-flying Allied planes and heard shooting close by. The prisoners were each given a raw potato and ordered into a nearby silo, where they took off their wet clothes and wrung them dry. The next day, April 25, they walked for about two hours until they were told to sit in a circle by the edge of a forest. From their vantage point, they saw tanks, trucks, and jeeps rolling by a little less than a mile away. Chuna assumed the vehicles were part of a German army unit. But then he noticed something unexpected—the guards and dogs had left the prisoners alone.

Soon a tank rumbled across the field directly toward the prisoners, who couldn't tell if it was friend or foe. At this point, Chuna, who was now 17 and weighed only 75 pounds, was almost too emotionally and physically drained to care.

The tank turned out to be from the US Army's 11th Armored Division and stopped five feet from the group. The hatch opened up and a curly-haired soldier popped out and announced, "We're Americans. You are now free!"

Chuna let the words sink in, savoring each one: "You . . . are . . . now . . . free!" *This is the happiest moment of my life,* he told himself. Then he closed his eyes and silently prayed, *Dear God, thank you for saving my life. But why did it take you so long to answer my prayers?*

After American medics treated Chuna's infected head wound, he was taken to the Zeilsheim DP (displaced persons) camp near Frankfurt, Germany. He learned that his mother, sisters Brondel and Rozia, and nieces and nephews had been murdered at the Treblinka death camp shortly after they were deported from Starachowice. He also discovered that his typhus-infected sister, Chaja, had been shot to death in Julag 1 along with other ill prisoners.

His cousin Ita, who had bandaged his head after the escape attempt in Julag 2, survived. With her help, Chuna was reunited with his brother Zachary, who had been in the Polish Army at the start of the war and had survived in the Vilna Ghetto (in what today is Vilnius, Lithuania). At the DP camp, Zachary sent a telegram to Diana, their sister in Washington, DC, notifying her that they had survived. In June 1946, Chuna and Zachary arrived in New York City, where, to their great surprise, they were met by their brother, David, who had fled during the German invasion. He had escaped to Lithuania and, using a false passport, went to Manchuria before reaching the United States in 1941.

David escorted Chuna and Zachary to their sister Diana's house. Eventually, Chuna, who Americanized his name to Henry Greenbaum, went into the dry-cleaning business in Washington and Maryland with Zachary. After Henry married, he and his wife, Shirley, raised four children. He has 12 grandchildren and 6 great-grandchildren.

After retiring from his successful business in 1997, Henry became a regular volunteer for the United States Holocaust Memorial Museum, speaking to groups throughout the country.

He credits his survival to perseverance, the will to live, a never-give-up attitude, and his strong faith in God. "We survivors thought the world would be more peaceful and friendlier after the Holocaust," he says. "But hate, discrimination, and anti-Semitism still exist. All we can do is tell you our stories, and maybe perhaps one day, discrimination and hate will end."

THE *SELEKTION* TERRORS

AGNES "AGI" LASZLO

(Agi Geva)

Every step was agony for 14-year-old Agi Laszlo. For weeks, she and 198 other female prisoners had been trudging in the frigid cold and bitter wind in the countryside of southern Germany. They had no boots, no coats, no hats, no underwear, just blankets draped over their paper-thin dresses that did little to ward off the brutal winter weather.

Under armed guard, the girls and women kept walking after being told that any day now they would meet up with a train that would take them the rest of the way to who knows where. Whatever the location, Agi figured it had to be better than slogging through wind-whipped snow, freezing rain, and icy mud in ill-fitting, worn-out shoes that left her feet bleeding and blistered.

Along the way, they had scavenged for food, sometimes from a farm where they found a raw cabbage, an old carrot, a potato. While crossing creeks, they had dropped to their knees to drink water out of their hands. During the day, the guards had made them sleep in barns and then march at night to avoid being seen.

With every mile they walked—and they had walked hundreds—Agi could feel her life slowly slipping away. She wondered how she would die. From hunger? From the cold? From fatigue?

Then one morning, after being herded into a drafty barn, the exhausted, starving women were told that they would reach the railway station the next day to meet the train. Agi felt a sense of relief. After an excruciating, dehumanizing two-month-long trek that had pushed her malnourished body beyond its limits, she had survived.

As Agi was resting, two girls in the barn began spreading terrifying news: "We overheard the guards," they whispered to the group. "They said the train is bringing them the guns and ammunition they need to execute us!"

Agi wondered how her life could have spiraled so abruptly into this wretched existence. Wasn't it just a year ago when she and her classmates were at her house studying for exams, making plans for a fun-filled summer, and rolling on the floor, laughing? Weren't they all so carefree and happy? Wasn't that what her life had been?

During her preschool days, Agi—that's what everyone called her instead of her birth name, Agnes—and her sister,

Zsuzsanna (Zsuzsi for short), who was a year younger, used to romp on a large farm outside the village of Pogony-Puszta, in Hungary. Her father, Zoltan, managed the farm, while their tall, redheaded mother, Rozsa, tended to the family and their beautiful, spacious house. The girls had no worries.

Then the Hungarian government fell under the influence of Nazi Germany and passed anti-Semitic laws, including one in 1936 that forbade Jews from holding management positions in agriculture. Distraught that he was fired for being Jewish, Zoltan suffered a heart attack from which he never fully recovered. Because Zoltan was in failing health, the burden of providing for the family fell on Rozsa's shoulders, so the Laszlos moved to Miskolc, Hungary, where she opened a small hotel.

Agi and Zsuzsi attended a Protestant gymnasium (a European term for "secondary school") because there were no Jewish schools in their neighborhood. Their father insisted they learn several languages because, he told them, "There might come a time when that knowledge will help you. It will give you power. If you learn other languages, no one can take that away from you." He arranged for tutors to teach them two languages he thought were the most important—German and English.

On March 19, 1944, when Agi was 13 and Zsuzsi was 12, their world turned upside down. Zoltan died. And on that same day, Germany occupied Hungary. The following day, after the funeral, the Laszlos saw armed German soldiers standing on street corners. Their presence didn't scare Agi because she was still in shock over her father's death. *Nothing can be worse than this*, she told herself.

The Nazis immediately laid down harsh anti-Semitic laws. Jews were ordered to wear the yellow Star of David and work in a labor brigade. They had to give up their bicycles to the municipality. Also, the government announced that those who swore loyalty to Hungary and worked in the fields would not be deported.

Willing to do anything to avoid deportation, Rozsa and the girls swore their allegiance to their country and then joined 30 others in a labor brigade. Before being sent to work on a small farm, the Laszlos were told to take whatever possessions they could carry. Agi stuffed her small valise with an heirloom watch, a book, personal items, scarves, a favorite dress, and a doll with wavy brown hair and eyes that opened and closed. There was no room for candy or food. Rozsa packed a bag with money, documents, family pictures, and jewelry. As an extra precaution, she also sewed money and valuables into the hem of her dress and the linings of her pockets.

On the farm, the three of them toiled in the fields from 5:00 a.m. until dark. For the first time in her young life, Agi's muscles and feet were constantly sore. *This can't get any worse*, she thought.

But then the pro-Nazi Hungarian government went back on its word to protect Jews in labor brigades. It sent gendarmes (Nazi soldiers serving as police) to round up the field workers and return them to Miskolc. On June 2, Agi's fourteenth birthday, she, Zsuzsi, Rozsa, and the others were marched into a fenced-in ghetto in Miskolc. Their new residence was a small apartment shared with six other families. The appallingly cramped space left everyone uncomfortable, stressed, and worried. Lack of food and water only made life more unbearable. *This must be the worst thing that can happen to us,* Agi thought. *Sweating all day in the fields was better than this.*

After a few weeks, they were transported to an open-air brick plant and told they would be going on a train ride. Agi was looking forward to it. She liked the comfy passenger trains, especially the times when she was munching on a sandwich in a window seat, watching the Hungarian countryside roll by. But when the locomotive steamed into the station, it pulled nothing but filthy cattle cars. *This can't be our train,* she thought. *They wouldn't put people in those disgusting cattle wagons.*

It *was* their train. Appalled by the cattle cars, the Jews balked, refusing to board. But they were no match for the armed guards and police who shoved men, women, and children into each hot, smelly boxcar before slamming and locking the doors.

As the train chugged out of Miskolc, panicky people screamed in hysterics. Hungry infants wailed. Bewildered children cried. Pregnant women fainted. The elderly were too dazed to utter a sound. Inside the dark boxcar, the air was thick and hard to breathe.

"It's not possible what's happening to us," Agi told her mother. "This isn't fit for humans. Even the cattle are given more space, and straw, too."

"Maybe we will be taken to a work camp out in the country," Rozsa said.

"I hope so, Anyu," Agi replied, using the Hungarian word for "Mom." "I'd be happier back in the ghetto—and I didn't think anything could be worse than the ghetto."

After three insufferable days in the cattle cars, they felt the train come to a stop. When the doors opened up, the prisoners—their legs wobbly from traveling so long—squinted in the light. They had arrived at Auschwitz.

For most, including Agi, the name Auschwitz meant nothing. They had no idea that it was a death camp where hundreds of thousands of Jews had already been exterminated in gas chambers made to look like showers. Agi didn't know that the smell reeking throughout the camp was from burning the bodies.

As the crowd moved slowly, Rozsa forced her way to the front and then worked back to the girls. "Listen carefully to me," she told them, looking rather shaken. "Don't ever call me Anyu and don't refer to yourselves as sisters. We must act like we are strangers to each other. The Nazis are splitting up families. When I was up to the front, I saw a young girl beg the officer, 'Please let me stay with my mother.' He immediately separated them. One went to the left and the other to the right."

Referring to the mother of Agi's best friend, Edith Rosenberg, Rozsa said, "I saw Mrs. Rosenberg get sent to the left and Edith to the right. I also noticed that old people and young children are sent left. I don't know what that means, but healthy ones who look over sixteen and younger than fifty are sent to the right. We must stay together."

Rozsa told the girls to pull out scarves from their bags. "You're no longer thirteen and fourteen years old," she told the girls. "You are now eighteen and nineteen. Under no circumstances do you say you are younger." She instructed them to put the scarves over their head and twist and tie them in a certain way to make themselves look older. Then Rozsa, who was 42, bound a scarf on her head differently in a style that was fashionable for younger people.

As the Laszlos inched in line toward the officer who was sending new arrivals to the left and right, Agi quivered in a fusion of disturbing emotions—depression, fear, anxiety. The possibility that she might be separated from her mother and sister was unbearable, and yet that's all she could think about. *If we're split up, I won't make it*, she told herself. In this frighteningly ghastly place where people were wailing and screaming, Agi was so scared she could barely shuffle forward.

Now it was the Laszlos' turn to stand in front of the officer. To Rozsa, he pointed to the right. To Zsuzsi, he pointed to the right. Agi took a step, and her little body tensed in dire suspense. The officer's index finger flicked up . . . and to the right. The unbridled relief Agi felt at that instant almost left her limp. She moved off and into the arms of her mother, happy they were all still together.

The joy was short-lived. *Kapos* began barking orders to the women to leave behind their bags, suitcases, and valises. Jews who kept their valuables in those bags protested. Some wept and some begged the guards to let them hold on to the bags. Agi was sad to surrender her valise, which contained items that were her only connection to home. Rozsa was much more upset because she had to give up the money that she planned to use as bribes to keep the three of them alive.

At least Anyu has money hidden in her dress, Agi thought.

Taken into a large room, the women and girls were ordered, "Undress and leave your clothes and shoes in the corner." Once again, many burst into tears. Like Rozsa, they had sewn money and valuables into their clothes. Now they would have nothing, nothing at all. Compounding their anguish, everyone stood totally nude. Agi had never felt so humiliated. She had never seen her mother naked and couldn't bear to look at her this way. *What will happen to us now?* she wondered.

The women were steered into another room, where all

hair was shaved off. Agi bit her lip to keep from crying when her long, beautiful braids were shorn. Agi and the others were told, "You will now get your showers." For those Jews who had been sent to the left earlier, *showers* meant the gas chamber. But the women sent to the right had yet to know about the atrocities at Auschwitz, so there was no panic when they heard the word *showers*. For them, water, not gas, poured out of the showerheads.

After washing themselves, they were sprayed with a disinfectant as if they were stray animals. The women were told to each pick out a prison-issued gray dress and a pair of shoes but weren't given any stockings or underwear. Nothing that Agi chose fit her. Each was given a bowl and two blankets and sent to a barrack, six people to a bunk that was nothing more than a wooden shelf.

To Agi, everything about Auschwitz was gray—the clothes, the barracks, the blankets, the constant haze, the smelly smoke belching from the chimneys. *What are they burning? Agi wondered. Why is there so much ash falling?* When Rozsa learned about Auschwitz's gas chambers and crematoriums, she pleaded with the other prisoners to keep those horrific details from her daughters. With plenty of reason to be petrified already, Rozsa didn't want her girls traumatized further by knowing the terrible truth.

The next day, Agi met up with her friend Edith. They had been the only two Jewish girls in their class back in Miskolc.

Rozsa told Edith, "You stay with us, and I will look after you like you are my own daughter."

Later that morning, covered transport trucks rumbled into the camp yard. Loudspeakers on the vehicles broadcast that all girls under the age of 16 would get better treatment, sleeping quarters, and food and should hop aboard the trucks. The announcement was tempting for many girls—including Agi, Zsuzsi, and Edith—who began heading toward the vehicles. Rozsa caught up with the three girls and turned them back. "You will not go into those trucks," she said sternly. "I don't care what the Nazis promise you. You will stay with me."

"But I miss my mother," Edith said. "If I go in the truck, it might take me to where my mother is."

No amount of reasoning by Rozsa could persuade Edith to remain with them. She ran to a truck and climbed aboard. Agi never saw her again.

Even though they felt like crying every day, Agi and Zsuzsi didn't because they knew it would break their mother's heart. And Rozsa didn't shed tears in front of them, wanting to appear strong for her daughters. She encouraged them day and night to be positive and brave, vowing, "As long as we stick together, we will survive."

Zsuzsi believed her, but Agi wasn't convinced. *We will never be free*, she thought.

Hopelessness and despair were contagious among the prisoners. One day, Agi saw a middle-aged woman scream, "I want to die! I want to die!" The inmate dashed toward the electrified wire fence to end her misery by electrocution. A guard saw her running and wanted to prolong her suffering, so just before the woman reached the fence to commit suicide, he turned off the electricity. Guards then hauled away the sobbing woman. *It's so cruel that she wasn't allowed to die,* Agi thought.

After about two weeks in Auschwitz, the Laszlos were put in a cattle car with others and transported to a different camp. On the one-day journey, Agi thought, *Thank goodness we are leaving. The next place can't possibly be any worse than Auschwitz. Where else but Auschwitz would prisoners try to kill themselves because they thought they were better off dead than alive?*

The train stopped at Plaszow, a slave labor camp near Krakow, Poland. The Laszlos soon learned that the camp housed not only thousands of Jews but also violent criminals, including murderers. Agi and Zsuzsi were terrified. From morning to evening, they were constantly looking over their shoulders, fearful that a homicidal inmate would attack them.

The Laszlos were given hard labor that was as senseless as it was degrading. At a stone quarry, they each had to carry big rocks up a hill for hours in the blazing sun. The following day, they had to bring those same rocks back down to where they found them. Zsuzsi, who turned 13 at Plaszow, didn't have the strength to haul large rocks up or down the hill, so she chose lighter ones to lug.

When a guard saw Zsuzsi carrying a rock smaller than

the others, he flew into a rage and began beating her. Agi and Rozsa were heartsick, but they knew better than to run to her aid, because that would have spelled doom for the entire family. So, through their tear-filled eyes, they had to watch in silence as the guard cruelly thrashed her.

"We're treated exactly as if we had gone back thousands of years in time, as if we were the slaves of Egypt," Agi complained. "I didn't think any place could be worse than Auschwitz, but now I know there is. It's here in Plaszow."

As the Red Army advanced toward Plaszow, officials began liquidating the camp. The Laszlos were among thousands of prisoners jammed into a long train of cattle cars. Not knowing where they were going, Agi and Zsuzsi struggled to contain their anxiety.

Trying to be positive, Rozsa told them, "Wherever we end up, it can't possibly be any worse than where we've been. It can only be better than Plaszow and Auschwitz. There is no worse place than those two."

Agi tried not to worry, tried to believe that they would arrive at a camp that was less evil, less vile. At day's end, the train stopped and the doors to the cattle cars opened. *Where are we this time?* Agi wondered, her view hidden by the prisoners in front of her. Unexpectedly, she heard a rising crescendo of moans and high-pitched wails from those exiting. When the Laszlos reached the opening and looked out, they gasped in horror.

They were back in Auschwitz.

"No! No! Tell me this isn't happening!" Agi cried out, her body seized with panic and fear. This time, Rozsa could not find any consoling words. There were none.

When the Laszlos stepped off the platform, they saw an impeccably dressed uniformed officer making a *Selektion* with the flick of his finger—some to the left, some to the right. What the prisoners didn't know was that the officer was Josef Mengele, the "Angel of Death," noted for choosing who would live as a slave laborer and who would die in the gas chamber. He gained his greatest notoriety as a physician who conducted grotesque and despicable experiments on prisoners.

Agi saw terror in her mother's eyes. The three of them looked in poor physical condition—rail thin, peeled sun-burned skin, sunken eyes. Of the trio, Agi was in the worst shape. Rozsa feared they would be considered unfit to work.

She told her daughters, "Follow me wherever I'm sent. If I'm chosen for work and you aren't, insist that you can work because the Germans need workers."

Trembling with apprehension, Rozsa went first. Mengele pointed to the right—the workers' side. Then Zsuzsi stood in front of him. He looked her up and down and directed her to the right. When it was Agi's turn, Mengele wasted no time in deciding this waif's fate. His finger pointed her to the left.

The frail girl refused to move. "No," Agi declared. Surprised that a lowly Jewish child would defy an officer of his stature, the armed soldiers leaned closer and aimed their weapons at her. In flawless German, Agi told him, "I want to go to the right."

"And why is that?" Mengele asked

"Because the people on the right can work."

"You don't look to me like you can work."

"Let me prove that I can," she said.

Mengele suddenly realized that the two of them were talking in German. "This is a Hungarian transport," he said. "And yet you speak German so well." Impressed by her command of the language, Mengele studied Agi for a moment and then gave a slight nod. "Go where you wish."

Just as her father, Zoltan, had said years earlier, language was power. It helped save Agi's life. She rushed to the right, only to find her mother lying on the ground. A minute earlier, Rozsa had seen Mengele point Agi to the left for extermination. Overcome with grief, Rozsa had fainted.

Shortly after Rozsa recovered, Agi fainted. It happened after she and the other surviving prisoners in her group were tattooed with numbers on their left arms. Having her identity reduced to a mere number—A18667—inscribed on her skin with indelible ink was humiliating and painful. Combined with the emotional strain of nearly being separated from her mother and sister, the stress caused Agi to pass out.

Day after day at Auschwitz, the Laszlos and their fellow inmates rose at 5:00 a.m. for *Appell* and stood for hours while guards repeatedly counted them. Agi was scared that at any moment she would be separated from her mother and sister, especially during the daily *Selektions* for various jobs. But somehow the threesome managed to stay together.

Bald, starving, and weak, Agi had all but given up hope of ever getting out of Auschwitz alive. Her spirits were almost nonexistent.

One dismal Sunday afternoon, she and the other glum prisoners were sitting outside, each too numb to even dream of freedom. Yearning for just a trace of joy in this joyless place, a small group went up to inmate Lili Bardos and asked her to sing. The tiny, spindly 24-year-old prisoner had been an opera singer from Agi's hometown of Miskolc. Lili declined. But they begged and pestered her until she finally gave in. She stood up and began to sing an aria. At first, she sounded shaky because she hadn't sung for so long. But with each note, her voice grew stronger and the aria grew more riveting.

The prisoners, who were slumped over with their heads down, suddenly perked up. Their bodies straightened and smiles filled their pale faces. The sheer beauty of her music lifted the souls of the entire camp—especially Agi's. Lili's arias from *La Bohème*, *Tosca*, and *Madama Butterfly* mesmerized Agi, whose dark mood turned brighter until it glowed with a renewed belief that life—even as bleak and fragile as one in Auschwitz—was still worth living.

From then on, Lili sang every Sunday afternoon, drawing

crowds of inmates and even the Nazi guards and officers. For the first time, Agi had something to look forward to in the camp, something to help get her through the dreary week.

In late fall, the Laszlos were among 180 Hungarian and 20 Polish women put in boxcars and transported out of Auschwitz. For the next three days, they suffered in extreme cold and had virtually nothing to eat or drink—dreadful conditions that made Agi worry she wouldn't survive the trip. Finally, they arrived at a small labor camp in Rochlitz, Germany.

For several weeks, the Laszlos were given special training in how to run various machines. For Agi, it was a relatively decent time. She was given the use of a chair, table, pencil, and paper—mundane things for those who were free, but treasured objects for a slave laborer who up until now had not been allowed to use them. Agi was learning something and exercising her brain—and she liked that. She felt as if she had a purpose; never mind that putting this new knowledge to work would help the Germans. It was better than Auschwitz, better than Plaszow.

When the training was over, the 200 women were sent to a factory that manufactured spare parts for airplanes in the German town of Calw. Any thought Agi had that the women would receive better treatment was quickly squelched. Given few breaks and little food, the slave laborers toiled 12 hours daily on the night shift from 7:00 p.m. to 7:00 a.m. in a factory that was big, noisy, and frightening. Agi and Zsuzsi operated a loud machine that made screws. While standing for hours on end throughout the night next to a machine that droned on and on, they constantly struggled to stay awake. One young worker fell asleep on the job, toppled into a machine, and was seriously injured. The laborers there never saw daylight. They weren't allowed to leave the building because the Nazis wanted to keep the Jewish slave laborers' presence secret from the outside world.

In February 1945, production at the factory came to a halt after one of the Jewish slave workers contracted typhus and eventually died. A week later, rumors circulated that the Allies were closing in on the Germans. Agi hoped that liberation was only days away.

But then the 199 surviving women were ordered out of the factory. Guarded by six soldiers, two officers, and a few female *Kapos*, they were sent on a brutal forced march in the dead of winter to meet up with a train.

For two weeks, then four, then six, they kept marching—and wasting away from little food and water. *Just when I thought it couldn't get any worse, it has*, Agi told herself. To her, this was no lengthy trek to a train. This was a death march. And she was resigned to dying.

Her strong-willed mother wasn't about to watch either daughter die. Rozsa tried to take their minds off their suffering by entertaining them with tales from books that she used to read to them at bedtime. She talked about the good times when the girls went to school and to the movies and swam and played with their friends. She reminded them of the days when food was plentiful and their house was filled with love and laughter. "When we go home—and we will go home—we'll once again have all that we've missed," she promised.

Agi wished that were true, but she was beyond believing. Part of her was ready to give up because it was a struggle to live. But she kept walking—sometimes leaning on Rozsa—because she didn't dare cause her mother any further heartache.

"Move faster!" the guards ordered the women. "If you want to meet the train, you'll have to walk at a quicker pace."

Agi hated the boxcars and cattle cars—some of her worst memories came from the ghastly conditions in them—and yet, as her frozen feet crunched through the snow, she wished she were on such a train.

After 240 miles (386 kilometers), Agi had lost her strength, her energy, and almost her will to live. So when the women were told they were close to the railway station, she was relieved—until word spread that the train carried the guns and ammunition that the guards planned to use to kill all of them. Reactions ranged from horror to acceptance to disbelief. Rozsa believed it was true, and her unbendable spirit suddenly went limp.

Agi broke down and wept. *I really don't care if I'm shot there or if I die here. I can't take another step. I just can't. I have nothing left in me.*

But where there was a spark of life, there was a flicker of hope. Still clinging to life, the women obediently got up the next morning and continued their march until they arrived at the railway station and collapsed from exhaustion.

The train wasn't there. After the guards had a lengthy meeting with authorities, a female *Kapo* told the women, "You missed the train. You'll have to keep walking."

Whatever the lowest point was that Agi had experienced over the past harrowing year, it didn't come close to matching how woefully miserable she felt now. *This is the worst day of my life. I'd rather die than take another step.* She had pushed her feeble body way past what she thought possible. Her brain no longer had the power to tell her legs to move.

But the last shred of survival instinct remaining in her gut was enough to coax her to trudge with the others for several hundred yards into a forest. Eventually, they looked around and noticed for the first time that the guards were gone. *Are we on our own?* Agi wondered.

The *Kapo* held up her hand and shouted, "Stop walking! Listen to me. From this moment on, the twenty-eighth of April, 1945 . . ." She hesitated because the next words were hard for her to say. "You are free."

Agi didn't know if she had heard correctly. It took a while before she realized that she truly was released from the clutches of the Nazis. *The worst day just turned into my best day!* Agi was bubbling with a happiness she hadn't experienced for such a long time that she didn't know what to say.

After the jubilation died down, someone said, "We are free. So now what? We are somewhere in southern Germany. It's cold. We have no food, no water. And the war is still going on. What do we do?"

Everyone had a different opinion. Eventually, the women broke into smaller groups and headed in separate directions. Under Rozsa's leadership, 30 mustered the strength to begin walking toward what they thought would be the Allies' position.

They soon heard voices in the woods. For several nerve-racking minutes, they worried German troops were closing in on them. But then Agi recognized some of the words. "They're speaking English!" she said excitedly. "They're Americans!"

Because she could speak the language, the group asked her to make contact with the soldiers. Someone earlier had found a stick with white fabric tied to it and handed it to Agi. She walked out and waved it.

The soldiers—the first Americans Agi had ever seen in person—stopped their advance. They were stunned to see emaciated, sick, weak, bald-headed women and girls standing in front of them. After Agi explained who they were and where they had come from, the soldiers brought them to their headquarters, which was a hotel in Plansee, Austria, just across the German border.

The Americans took pity on the women. After providing them with food, water, and medical care, the soldiers said, "What can we get for you?" Some of the women yearned for schnitzel and cookies. Others wanted stockings and blouses. After looking in the mirror and seeing her pasty face, gaunt cheeks, and hairless head, Agi thought, *I know what might help.*

She asked for lipstick.

After the war, Agi, Zsuzsi, and Rozsa spent eight months recovering in Innsbruck, Austria, before returning to their hometown of Miskolc, Hungary. They, along with opera singer Lili Bardos and Lili's sister, also named Zsuzsi, were among only 105 of the city's more than 10,000 deported Jews who reportedly survived the Holocaust. One who didn't make it was Agi's best friend, Edith Rosenberg, who was an Auschwitz victim. None of her other Jewish friends survived, either.

Rozsa discovered that neighbors had taken all the furniture and fixtures from her hotel after her deportation, so she went to the municipality for help. Accompanied by local officials, Rozsa went throughout the neighborhood and retrieved much of the stolen items. Then she reopened the hotel.

In 1949, Agi and Zsuzsi emigrated to Israel. Later that same year, Rozsa married the family's widowed attorney, who had lost his wife and six-year-old son in the Holocaust.

Zsuzsi, who wed a Holocaust survivor, settled at Haogen, an

Israeli kibbutz (a communal farm) and has lived there ever since, taking the name Shosha Granot. She has 3 children, 13 grandchildren, and 17 great-grandchildren, all living in Israel.

In 1956, Rozsa and her husband were allowed to leave communist Hungary. The couple went to live at the same kibbutz as Shosha, where Rozsa remained until her death in 1999 at the age of 97.

Agi raised two children and became a successful insurance broker in Israel. After living there for 53 years, she moved to the United States to be near her daughter in Maryland. Agi, who has four grandchildren and four great-grandchildren, makes yearly trips to Israel to see her son, grandchildren, great-grandchildren, sister, and relatives.

She has been volunteering at the United States Holocaust Memorial Museum since 2002, speaking to schools, groups, and organizations. "My mother and my sister wanted so much to forget about the Holocaust," she says. "After liberation, Anyu told us, 'You are alive. You are free. There's no reason to talk about it.' So we never discussed it. Years later, when I heard people say the Holocaust never happened, I knew I had to speak. My eight-year-old granddaughter in Israel suggested I should talk to her class about the Holocaust. That was the first time I spoke about it. Since then, I've made it my mission to talk about the Holocaust. It's hard for me, but it's something I have to do because everybody should know what happened and how it happened."

SLOW MURDER

NIUTEK FRAJMAN

(Norman Frajman)

Niutek Frajman could not escape seeing death. It was everywhere, every day in the Warsaw Ghetto.

In the streets, sidewalks, and alleys, the young boy would see victims of slow murder—the Jews who had died from rampant typhus or from starvation, which the Nazis cruelly engineered.

There wasn't a day when Niutek didn't spot someone picking up a corpse out of the gutter and placing it on a handcart piled with other victims who had died during the night . . . or notice a body, covered with newspapers, in a wagon pulled by a family member to the cemetery for burial in a mass grave . . . or pass a distraught mother clutching her dead baby, unwilling to let go of her lifeless bundle.

On so many street corners, Niutek would see people begging for food—many who were barefoot toddlers and others who were grown-ups in the final throes of malnutrition, their faces yellow and puffy and their bellies swollen. He could tell they, too, would soon be corpses.

Occasionally, Niutek would encounter bodies of victims, who, in a sad sense, were considered the lucky ones because they had died quickly. They were the Jews fatally beaten up on a whim by German soldiers and Polish police or randomly shot by Nazis roaring down the street on motorcycles that had sidecars with mounted machine guns.

The daily dose of gruesome sights aged Niutek way beyond his years, which was what happened to kids like him who had a good heart and an innocent soul. Such was life—or rather death—in the Warsaw Ghetto.

In September 1939, just days before Niutek's tenth birthday, German forces mercilessly bombed Warsaw, Poland, causing a mass evacuation. After securing their well-appointed apartment, the Frajmans—Niutek; his father, Leon, who was a successful businessman; mother, Hela; and eight-year-old sister, Renia—fled to the town of Kovel in eastern Poland, which fell under Soviet occupation.

After staying there through the winter, Leon received reports that the Germans were not mistreating the Jews of Warsaw as badly as he had feared. Not wanting to live like refugees any longer, he decided that the family should return to their city. But the Russians weren't allowing anyone to leave their borders. So Leon hired a guide who agreed to help the family sneak back into the German-controlled sector of Poland.

The guide eventually brought the Frajmans to a barbed wire fence that blocked access to the German side. As the guide was cutting a hole for them, they were caught at gunpoint by Russian guards, who tossed everyone into jail for two days.

On the third day, a Russian official released Niutek, Renia, and Hela and literally shoved them across the border. But Leon remained imprisoned, leaving the family to wonder if he would ever be reunited with them. Once freed, the trio headed to Warsaw on a train designated for Jews only—an ominous sign of anti-Semitism. But Niutek naïvely thought it was great. "We have our own railroad," he crowed. "How much better does it get?"

When they arrived home, everything had changed. They were relieved their 40-unit apartment building, which was owned by Niutek's grandparents, had not been damaged during the bombing. But their apartment had been plundered of all its expensive furniture and possessions and was now occupied by Jews who had been deported from Germany. The Frajmans were forced to live in just one of the rooms of their former residence with the strangers. Meanwhile, Leon's thriving transportation business had been seized by the Nazis and given to a *Volksdeutsche*, the term for a German who didn't live in Germany.

When Niutek went to play with his non-Jewish friends, who had been his classmates and soccer teammates before the war, they turned on him, calling him Jew Boy, and beat him up for no reason. He found himself isolated from his former pals and could no longer attend school.

In fall 1940, shortly after Niutek turned 11, he, Hela, Renia, and the 350,000 other Jewish residents of Warsaw were forced to move into a designated area, which German authorities sealed off from the rest of the city. The heavily guarded ghetto was enclosed by a 10-foot-tall wall topped with broken glass and barbed wire. Any Jew caught outside the ghetto without special permission was executed.

By the following year, more than 450,000 Jews, including those from nearby towns, were squeezed into a small area of 1.3 square miles (3.4 square kilometers). The apartments and houses were so crammed that each tiny room became the living quarters for, on average, seven people.

Having a job was vital to survival. While Hela worked at a factory that manufactured parts for German warplanes, Niutek was a messenger boy at a Nazi-run distribution center. Because he was required to live with his fellow workers at the center, he saw his mother and sister only occasionally.

Those who held jobs could get ration cards to buy food. But Renia was too young for work, so Hela had to share her meager food allotment with her. The Nazis had severely limited the rations of bread and vegetables so that the supply of food wasn't nearly enough to sustain life for the Jews. Their stomachs were always empty, always craving anything edible.

Niutek worked at the *Umschlagplatz*, or collection point. Supplies from the Aryan, or non-Jewish, side of the city were delivered and off-loaded onto platforms and then distributed in the ghetto. Trucks brought in food—if you could call it that—which usually consisted of rotten vegetables that were originally destined for the garbage. Whenever he helped unload the trucks, Niutek would swipe a potato, carrot, or beet and stuff it in his pants. Then, the next time he saw his mother and sister, he would share it with them.

He knew he risked execution if he were caught stealing. It was the same punishment for those captured sneaking in or out of the ghetto. But Niutek would leave the ghetto anyway to find food, as many child smugglers did. It was safer to do it during the daytime because Jews were not allowed outside at night after curfew. In the Nazi mind-set, there was never a valid excuse to break curfew. Niutek's cousin Lolek was on a work detail for the Germans, removing garbage from the ghetto and taking it outside the walls. Through no fault of his own, Lolek was delayed and didn't return to the ghetto on his horse-drawn wagon until after curfew. He was shot and killed on his way home.

Niutek felt an obligation to take risks for his mother and sister. Having no news about his father—possibly executed, possibly imprisoned—the boy told himself, *Mama and Renia had depended on Papa, but now it's up to me. I am the man of the family.*

Before slipping through one of several secret openings in the ghetto wall next to a cemetery, Niutek would take off his white armband with the blue Star of David that every Jew was required to wear in public. On the Aryan side of the wall, he would pretend to be a non-Jew and walk to his former neighborhood even though he feared someone would recognize him. He would enter a store and buy food with money that Hela had squirreled away.

To avoid any suspicion that he was smuggling food into the ghetto, he would tie the cuffs of his pants tightly around his ankles and drop food inside his pant legs. Then he would slip through the opening in the ghetto wall and deliver the food to his mother and sister. His arrival was always a cause for celebration for two reasons: He completed his mission without being caught, and he helped his family fight off hunger for another day.

Other brave Jews smuggled food and medicine into the ghetto, but the death toll from starvation and disease kept rising. By June 1942—a year and a half after the ghetto was created—an estimated 83,000 Jews had perished, most by slow murder.

Niutek felt terrified every minute of every day. He would go to work in the morning always wondering if he would return alive that evening. In the back of his mind lurked the constant worry that he or his mother or sister would be struck down by a bullet or a fatal illness.

In summer 1942, the Nazis promised ghetto residents a better life—more food, improved housing, school for the children—if they agreed to be transported by train to a work camp in the countryside. Those who accepted would also receive three pounds of bread and a pound of marmalade. For thousands of starving Jews, this offer sounded great, so they volunteered.

Within a week or so, some of them sent letters to family members in the ghetto, saying they were enjoying this new work camp. No one in the ghetto knew exactly where it was. So members of the Jewish underground followed the freight cars that were carrying the Jews. The train stopped about 60 miles (97 kilometers) northeast of Warsaw at a place called Treblinka. Upon further investigation, the underground discovered this so-called work camp was really an extermination camp where thousands of new arrivals were being gassed and cremated daily. The letters received by family members praising the "work camp" were nothing but lies written by victims coerced at gunpoint to lure more people out of the ghetto and into one of the Nazis' most notorious death camps.

When members of the resistance reported to ghetto residents tales of horror about Treblinka, many Jews refused to believe it. A common reason for denial: "It's impossible for a cultured people like the Germans to be capable of carrying out such atrocities." Because their judgment was clouded by hunger and illness, many Jews continued to trust the devious Nazi propaganda and went willingly on the transports.

But the majority grew to believe the shocking reports of mass murder. When the number of volunteers shrank, the SS, with the help of Polish police and anti-Semitic civilians, began forcibly deporting about 6,000 to 7,000 Jews from the ghetto every day. It was clear to Niutek that the trains weren't taking them to a better life but to an awful death.

In July, while working at the *Umschlagplatz*, Niutek was snared in a roundup of workers marked for deportation. While soldiers gathered more people, Niutek and his comrades were held in a locked fifth-floor room of a building next to a warehouse where he worked. Without any hope of escape, the petrified boy thought, *We're doomed.*

But, speaking in a low voice so the armed guards on the other side of the door couldn't hear, an older slave laborer said, "I think there's a way out of here." Pointing to a wooden plank, he said, "That looks long enough to reach from the window here to the windowsill of the building next door. Let's put it out there and have someone walk across it and open the window on the other building. Then all of us can go across one at a time and save ourselves." Turning to Niutek, the man said, "You're the youngest one here and the most agile, so you're the best person to go over first and open the window."

Niutek was scared, knowing so many bad things could happen to him. He could fall or get shot or the board could break. But the chance to escape—which seemed impossible just moments earlier—had trumped his fear.

Quietly, they maneuvered the plank until it spanned the distance between the buildings and rested on the two windowsills opposite each other. Taking a deep breath, Niutek carefully got on the plank on his hands and knees and began crawling across it. The board bent and creaked and wobbled. As he inched his way toward the other side, he kept mentally blocking the image of him plunging to his death.

Niutek didn't dare look down and hoped no one on the ground looked up. But someone did. When he was about two-thirds of the way across, he was spotted by the Polish police, who began shooting at him. As bullets zipped past him, he quickened his crawl, reached the sill, opened the window, and tumbled inside.

I made it! he thought. *And I wasn't hit.* He had entered a warehouse floor filled with furniture that the Nazis had confiscated from Jews who had been deported. When he found a large wardrobe, he thought, *This will be a perfect place to hide.* He opened its double doors, stepped inside, and closed them. He didn't budge, convinced that the police would be searching the floor for him. He kept listening for footsteps or any sounds indicating someone was nearby. He heard nothing.

Maybe the police aren't searching for me. But the silence also meant that his fellow workers didn't make it across.

As the hours ticked by, Niutek tried to keep his nerves in check and figure out his next move. *Do I stay hidden or do I try to get out?* By evening, shortly before curfew, he worked up the nerve to open the wardrobe. Cautiously, he stepped out, crept down the stairway, and made his way undetected to the home of his uncle and grandparents, who lived close by.

Niutek eventually found another job elsewhere in the ghetto. Renia, who was too young to work, needed to stay completely out of sight to avoid being deported, so she hid behind a false wall in the apartment while Hela was at the factory.

On September 12, 1942, the day after Niutek turned 13, the Nazis temporarily stopped the mass deportations to Treblinka. About 365,000 Jews from the ghetto had been exterminated there and an additional 35,000 had been murdered within the ghetto walls. An estimated 70,000 Jews, including the Frajmans, remained in the Warsaw Ghetto.

In January 1943, the Nazis planned to deport all able-bodied residents to work camps near Lublin, Poland, and send the rest to their deaths at Treblinka. But armed resistance by Jews in the ghetto halted the operation after only three days.

Emboldened by their success, Jewish fighters sneaked out of the ghetto and purchased arms and made their own explosives. They also built more than 600 underground bunkers and shelters to prepare for an uprising against the next attempt to liquidate the ghetto.

No one had any illusions that they could hold off the German forces forever. This would be a suicide mission. As one fighter told Niutek, "We're all going to die, but not without a struggle. We want people to know that the Jews didn't go like lambs to the slaughter. What better way to die than with a weapon in your hands?" Niutek pleaded with the leaders to let him join the resistance, but they told him he was too young.

On April 19, the eve of Passover, German forces showed up, triggering the Jewish rebellion within the ghetto. Running from rooftop to rooftop, firing old weapons, and hurling Molotov cocktails, 750 resisters fought with passion. But they were overwhelmed by heavy artillery, daily aerial bombings, and a massive number of troops who, by going from building to building, reduced the ghetto to flaming rubble and snuffed out the uprising.

During the early days of the conflict, Niutek, Hela, and Renia hid behind the false wall in the apartment while 6,500 residents were either killed or sent to Treblinka for immediate extermination. By the end of the uprising, another 56,000 Jews were put on transports bound for various work camps. The Frajmans were among them, stuffed in a boxcar packed with 120 fellow Jews—so many that it was impossible to sit down or crouch; they all had to stand. Each boxcar had a five-gallon bucket of water for drinking and an empty one for use as a toilet.

The floors of the cars had been sprayed with chlorine disinfectant. But the fumes made it difficult to breathe and caused extreme thirst. The water was quickly consumed, and soon, parched throats left some people crazed. Niutek saw a man swipe the sweat off another person's face with his fingers just to moisten his lips. Niutek was so dehydrated and desperate for any kind of liquid that he resorted to drinking his own urine.

By the time the train reached its final destination of Lublin on the third day of the journey, 12 people had died in the Frajmans' boxcar.

Met with angry shouts and threats from armed soldiers with snarling guard dogs, the Jews were marched in five columns about two miles (three kilometers) to a field outside the Majdanek (pronounced my-DON-ik) concentration camp and kept there overnight. Signs around the camp's electrified fence warned that the ground outside was mined. The camp covered 667 acres and contained 22 barracks, 19 watchtowers, 7 gas chambers, 2 gallows, and a crematorium.

In the morning, the *Selektion* began as an SS officer pointed his thumb to the left or right. Left meant life. Right meant death for anyone who limped, wore glasses, had gray hair, was pregnant, or was considered unable to work. They were put in trucks and never seen again.

Fortunately, the Frajmans were considered useful. But then, men and women were abruptly separated. It happened so fast that Niutek never had a chance to say good-bye to his mother and sister.

Before the 13-year-old boy could come to grips with now being completely on his own, he found out that, here in this field, evil knew no bounds. He witnessed sadistic guards— many of them anti-Semitic Ukrainians and Lithuanians—pull children out of line and shoot them right in front of their horrified parents. As if that weren't despicable enough, the guards switched their vile tactics and selected certain parents and executed them in front of their shocked children.

Niutek and about 1,000 men and teenagers were marched into the camp, all the while abused by psychotic *Kapos* who took pleasure in beating and whipping them. Forced to strip, the new prisoners were shaved of all body hair and sent to the showers. Next, a smelly, oil-based disinfectant known as creosote was applied with a large paintbrush to all shaved areas, including the head, which left everyone's skin with a burning sensation. Each prisoner was then assigned a number and given a striped uniform that was either too big or too small, a thin jacket, pants, and wooden clogs. When Niutek glanced at his fellow inmates, they didn't even look human to him;

more like bald clowns in a nightmarish circus. *And I'm one of them*, he thought.

They were led to their quarters, Barrack 21, which had three-level bunks designed for about 100 inmates but now was shelter for 400 men. Each prisoner was given a lice-infested blanket and a canvas bag, which he filled with straw to make a mattress. Like the others, Niutek had to sew his new identity number onto his jacket.

Among the camp's harsh rules: Whenever a red light was on in the barrack, you could not go outside; if you did, you were shot. If you stayed longer than three minutes in the open-air latrine, you received a vicious clubbing. If you repeatedly violated the time limit, you would be thrown into the latrine pit to drown. Committing a minor infraction would cost you 25 lashes with a whip on your backside, which you had to count out loud. If you lost count, you had to start over from number one. You couldn't commit suicide because if you threw yourself on the electrified fence, other prisoners would be selected for punishment. As one *Kapo* hissed to the inmates, "You don't have the right to take your own life. Only we can kill you. That's our privilege."

Every day, the inmates were awakened at 3:30 a.m. for *Appell*. After their breakfast of a tasteless coffee brewed from wheat, they were put into work groups of 30 to 40 men and marched to a work site. There they loaded bricks in wheelbarrows and, while keeping up a running pace and under constant harassment, carried them to a designated spot and unloaded them. At noon, the prisoners were marched back to camp for another body count and lunch, which was typically boiling-hot disgusting slop or soup. Because they weren't given spoons, the inmates often burned their lips, so a spoon became a treasured item. Often before they had a chance to finish, the whistle blew and they had to dump the soup and run back to work. At 6:00 p.m., they returned to camp, where they were counted and given rations, which consisted of a two-pound loaf of bread for every 16 people. Once a week, the prisoners received a quarter-pound of margarine for every 20 people. Niutek never ate his margarine. He spread it on certain parts of his body because he suffered from eczema, a disease that causes cracked, dry skin to become swollen, itchy, and inflamed.

To Niutek, every minute in Majdanek felt like living under a death sentence. Life meant nothing to the guards and *Kapos*, who tried to find any excuse—not that they needed one—to beat, whip, maim, or kill prisoners. There was no limit to the depravity practiced in the camp.

"There is absolutely no hope of ever getting out of here," Niutek lamented to a comrade.

"There is one way out," said the prisoner. "It's through the chimney of the crematorium. No matter how you die—whether you're shot or electrocuted or commit suicide—you will be cremated, and only your ashes will be free."

In October 1943, after enduring six dreadful months at Majdanek, Niutek, who had just turned 14, got a lucky break—if moving from one concentration camp to another can be considered lucky. When a train arrived to transport 3,000 prisoners, Niutek pushed his way into the crowd and onto a boxcar. They were taken to a slave labor camp in the Polish city of Skarzysko-Kamienna (pronounced skar-JISH-ko kam-e-EN-ah), where they were put to work for the Nazis making bullets and grenades in an arms factory.

Niutek's first assignment there, however, was to join two other prisoners in applying creosote—in this case as a preservative—to a watchtower. For several days, the men were painting while suspended on ropes in bitter cold and howling wind in only their threadbare clothes. As difficult as it was for him to carry out his job when his skin was freezing from the winter weather and stinging from the creosote, Niutek was fortunate he wasn't in Majdanek.

On November 3, just a few weeks after he had left that camp, the remaining 18,400 Jews were marched out in large groups and machine-gunned to death, falling into trenches they had been forced to dig earlier. To drown out the noise of the horrific carnage, the Nazis blared classical music over loudspeakers. The mass killing was part of *Aktion Erntefest* (German for "Operation Harvest Festival"), the largest single-day Nazi massacre of Jews in the entire war. More than 42,000 Jews were murdered in Lublin-area concentration camps in a coordinated slaughter led by SS troops and Ukrainian guards.

A few weeks later, Niutek, who was feeble from hunger and exposure, contracted typhus. Suffering from a high fever and barely conscious, he was brought to the hospital, which, he knew, was one step removed from being executed. As he expected, guards labeled him a nonproductive Jew and selected him for death along with several other patients. However, before a truck arrived to haul the condemned away, friend and fellow inmate David Reischer, a carpenter in his twenties, sneaked into the infirmary. He walked Niutek out and hid him under a pile of wood shavings in a workshop. Because the camp didn't conduct a head count, the guards didn't realize that Niutek was missing.

Once the *Selektion* for nonproductive Jews was over, Niutek returned to his bunk and slowly regained enough strength to work. "I owe you my life," he told David. "I will never forget what you did for me."

Although friendships were not common in concentration camps, Niutek formed a strong bond with David. For a lonely and frightened boy who had no news of his family's fate, it felt comforting to have an older person looking out for him. They helped each other survive. One day, while Niutek was marching to work, a kindhearted German civilian came up to him and handed him a sandwich, which the boy tucked into his pants. Even though he was starving and wanted to devour the whole thing, he gave half of it to David.

Then came a devastating blow. Niutek learned that his mother, Hela, and sister, Renia, had been gassed and cremated at Majdanek a year earlier. He would later learn that Renia contracted tuberculosis and was spitting up blood. During a *Selektion*, she was pegged a nonproductive Jew. Hearing Renia crying, Hela, who still was strong enough to remain a slave laborer, wanted to spare the 12-year-old girl the anguish of dying alone. Hela left the workers group and joined her daughter on the doomed side. She took Renia by the hand, knowing full well that in a few minutes they would be led to the gas chamber. The only comfort Niutek took from their deaths was that they had died together.

The loss of his mother and sister—he still didn't know what had happened to his father—broke Niutek's spirit. He mindlessly carried out his work in a robotlike existence at the Skarzysko camp through the winter and spring of 1944 and into summer.

On August 5, he and hundreds of other prisoners were shipped to the Buchenwald concentration camp near Weimar, Germany. There, Niutek was registered as prisoner 68616 and given a new striped prison uniform. He was soon transferred to Schlieben, a satellite camp, where he was assigned to a factory that made bazookas.

About three weeks after his arrival, an American bombing raid destroyed a nearby armaments factory and railroad tracks, killing nearly 100 prisoners and wounding a few hundred more. SS officers arrived and supervised the reconstruction of the factory and rails, using slave laborers like Niutek. Constantly yelling, *"Mach schnell!"* (German for "Hurry up!"), the officers and guards whipped and struck the prisoners, working them to death—in many cases literally—day and night. When the weather turned wintry, Niutek was helping lay track. Working without gloves, his hands sometimes froze to the steel rails, leaving him with frostbitten fingers.

He and the other prisoners toiled while suffering hunger pains that wrenched their stomachs. Food, anything that he could swallow to curb the nagging bellyache, was foremost in Niutek's mind—that, and the dream of one day being free.

In spring 1945, as the Red Army gained ground on the retreating German soldiers, the Nazis began emptying out Schlieben. Niutek was among hundreds of inmates taken away in freight cars before being separated into smaller groups. Surrounded by armed SS troops, Niutek's group was marched from town to town and made to dig antitank ditches. Almost daily, he watched fellow inmates drop dead from exhaustion, hunger, or exposure. Some who couldn't shovel fast enough were pushed aside and shot.

For a month, every day was the same: march to a location, dig deep trenches, sleep in the woods or barns, get up, go to a new location, dig ditches. *When will this ever end?* Niutek wondered. *Probably when I die.*

Outside of a small town on the Germany-Czechoslovakia border, the prisoners were put up for the night in a school-house. When they woke up the next morning, they discovered the guards had disappeared. At first, the inmates were suspicious this was some kind of trick, and that the moment they stepped outside, they would be shot.

But later that morning, Polish armed forces, under the direction of Russian officers, arrived and announced the prisoners had been liberated. The soldiers treated them warmly and shared their skimpy field rations with them.

The day Niutek had dreamed about for years had finally turned into reality. Feeling alive—really alive for the first time since the German invasion—the 15-year-old boy walked into the nearest church. He didn't care that it was Christian and he was Jewish. He kneeled down and said a little prayer that started with "Thank you, God, for letting me live."

He later asked a soldier, "What date is it?"

"May eighth," the soldier responded.

Niutek said, "From now on, I will consider May eighth a second birthday because today is the date when I start a new life."

After he was liberated, Niutek went to Prague, Czechoslovakia, seeking news of any family survivors, and then lived in the Russian zone in occupied Germany, where he worked as an interpreter, translating German into Russian. He eventually reached a displaced persons camp in the American zone near Berlin, Germany, and got in touch with an uncle who was living in the United States. In 1948, Niutek, who was 19 and didn't speak English, emigrated to New York.

To his great shock, Niutek, who changed his name to Norman, learned that his father, Leon, was alive and living in Israel. Following the Frajmans' arrest in 1940 in Poland for trying to cross the border from the Russian sector to the German sector, Leon had been sent to a prison in Siberia, where he had survived under harsh conditions, including near-starvation. After the war, the Soviet Union had declared an amnesty for imprisoned Polish citizens. Upon his release, Leon had returned to Poland, then had gone to Israel and remarried. He and Norman made contact, and in 1962, Leon came to the United States for an emotional visit with Norman—whom he hadn't seen in 22 years—and Norman's wife, Shelley.

Norman built a successful textile business with retail stores on Long Island. He and Shelley raised two children and now have two grandchildren.

Norman remained close friends with fellow Holocaust survivor David Reischer, who had also emigrated to New York. Decades later, when David was dying of cancer and placed in hospice care, Norman remained by his bedside until his death, a devoted friend forever grateful that David had saved his life at the Skarzysko concentration camp.

Over the years, Norman compiled a list of 126 names of relatives who were murdered by the Nazis. "How did I survive? It was an act of providence and nothing else," says Norman today. "I wasn't stronger or smarter than those who died. I feel some higher being was watching over me. For all intents and purposes, I should be dead. The older I get, the more I realize why I was spared—to share the story of the tragedy of mankind."

Retiring in 1998, Norman moved with Shelley to Boynton Beach, Florida, where he became president of the Child Survivors/ Hidden Children of the Holocaust of Palm Beach County. For years, he has been speaking at schools throughout the area, bringing with him the striped uniform he first wore at Buchenwald as a symbol of the atrocities he endured.

Norman has returned to Poland three times through the March of the Living tours for educators and Jewish teenagers. "I went back to Poland, to places that had memories of tragedy," he says. "It didn't hit me until I saw the crematorium at Majdanek [where his mother and sister were murdered]. I fell apart and cried bitterly. It took a lot out of me."

During a Polish trip in 2003, Norman, at age 73, was bar mitzvahed at a synagogue near Auschwitz in a spur-of-the-moment ceremony, having missed out on the ritual for 13-year-old Jewish boys because of his imprisonment during the Holocaust.

He also never had a chance to return to school. In 2014, at age 84, Norman attended graduation ceremonies, where the School District of Palm Beach County presented him with an honorary high school diploma. "We treasure and love Norman for his commitment to Holocaust education," said Maureen Carter, Holocaust Studies Program Planner for the school district.

"Miracles do happen in a person's life," Norman said at the time. "This is one of them. I believe that while standing on the stage surrounded by well-wishers, I received the graduation diploma in the name of all of the young people whose voices were silenced."

Today, Norman continues to tell students about his horrific experiences because, he says, young people must know what hate is capable of creating. "Get rid of the four-letter word 'hate,'" he says. "This created a great catastrophe that I cannot forgive or forget. But I can never become a hater. Otherwise Hitler would win because he would have made me one.

"We must concentrate on doing away with hatred and bullying. We must leave a legacy for future generations to learn to live in peace and harmony. Today's young people are more receptive to this message than any other generation. They will never permit another Holocaust. In their hands, we are in for a better tomorrow."

UNDER THE NAZI NOOSE

RACHEL MUTTERPERL

(Rae Goldfarb)

※

Nine-year-old Rachel Mutterperl was crouched in the family's dark, secret hiding place, trying to picture the terrifying scenes outside. Angry shouts. Frightened wails. Pounding footsteps. Sporadic gunfire. Breaking glass. Anguished moans.

All around her, mayhem raged in the streets of the Jewish ghetto in Dokszyce, Poland, as armed Nazis ran wild. In their bloodthirsty drive to hunt down their prey, the unrelenting Nazis were on a door-to-door rampage, seizing victims and marking them for death.

For days and days, Rachel had remained concealed in a cramped two-and-a-half-foot-wide space between two walls in the back of her house. With her were her six-year-old brother, Shlomo, mother, grandmother, and two other children. There was nothing to say. There was nothing to do—except hope and pray they wouldn't be discovered, unlike so many other hidden Jews who had been captured.

The awful sounds outside would die down and then rise again to nerve-jangling pitches. More screaming. More howling. More shooting. It seemed the massacre would never end.

After an unbearable week or more confined between the walls—Rachel had lost track of time—she and the others heard footsteps and voices coming from inside the house. The walls rattled from the sounds of doors opening and closing and furniture being moved. Were Germans searching for them? Were local non-Jews looting the house? It was impossible to tell from the hiding place.

Now the footsteps and voices were becoming louder—an indication the intruders were drawing closer to them. Rachel and the others remained perfectly still, barely breathing. The next few excruciating minutes would determine if they lived another day . . . or died today.

Compared to most kids in Dokszyce (pronounced dok-SHIZ-see), Rachel and Shlomo enjoyed a privileged childhood. Their parents, Beryl and Dina, both Orthodox Jews, were successful in business and often brought home gifts for the kids. Beryl bought products such as apples, grain, and flaxseed that he exported to Germany; he also provided meat to a nearby Polish army garrison. Dina owned a thriving fabric store, which was next to Beryl's butcher shop in front of their large home in the bustling Jewish section of the town (now known as Doksycy, Belarus).

Most everyone in the region liked the couple, who traveled extensively and treated their customers as friends. If farmers were financially strapped, Beryl often paid them in advance. Because of their business dealings, the couple had many gentile friends and acquaintances and once even invited a Greek Orthodox priest over for Passover.

An infection claimed Beryl's life in 1937 when Rachel was five and Shlomo was two, so Dina took over his business while managing her own. She had help running the house, including a non-Jewish nanny who looked after the kids, mostly Shlomo. Because Dina placed a premium on education, Rachel had a Jewish governess who taught her to read by age three. The little girl could also paint and speak Hebrew, Yiddish, and Polish.

On the morning of September 18, 1939, Rachel, who was a few months from turning seven, awakened to a frightening roar as tanks and other military vehicles of the Red Army rumbled into the town. Day and night for a whole week, a steady stream of invading Soviet troops rolled through Dokszyce as they began to occupy all of eastern Poland.

Denouncing capitalists like Dina, the Russians campaigned against prosperity and began taking over family businesses. Dina reacted quickly by distributing her fabric to customers and giving away clothing to farmers with the understanding that they would provide her with food or other necessities if the need arose; the rest they could keep for themselves. She buried gold coins and jewelry in her yard so the Russians couldn't steal them. Dina figured the valuables could be used to pay bribes or ransom if she or her children were in trouble.

Less than two years later, Germany controlled all of Poland. On July 3, 1941, German soldiers marched into Dokszyce and immediately demolished Jewish buildings, burned the Torah scrolls and the holy books, and destroyed the tombstones in the Jewish cemetery.

Polish gentiles began pointing out to the Germans which Jews had cooperated with the Russians. Those Jews were summarily executed and their homes looted. To instill further fear, the Nazis rounded up 50 Jews, marched them to a sand pit, and made them watch as a soldier shot and killed an innocent little boy. Later, the Nazis took about 30 Jewish men and, while beating them with sticks, forced them to clean and scrape manure off the streets with their bare hands.

On September 22, which was Rosh Hashanah—an important Jewish holiday—the Nazis marched eight Jews to the Jewish cemetery, made them dig their own graves, and shot them. Among the victims was Leah Blokh, a teenage girl who, seconds before she was killed, shouted to her executioners, "Do not think, you murderers, that you will win the war. No! Our spilled blood will take revenge upon you!"

German authorities required the Mutterperls and other Jewish families to wear yellow badges on the front and back of their garments to identify them as Jews. Christian children spit on Rachel and called her names whenever she was outside, so she didn't venture far from home. If she was on the sidewalk and a gentile approached from the opposite direction, Rachel had to step off until that person passed. Sometimes, kids pushed her out of the way.

In November 1941, the Nazis sectioned off a portion of Dokszyce and turned it into a Jewish ghetto. Those Jews who lived elsewhere in town were forced into the ghetto and told to find their own living arrangements. Rachel and her family didn't need to move because their house was inside the ghetto. But many uprooted Jews were in desperate need of living quarters, so the Mutterperl house became packed with relatives and other families. It was so crowded that Rachel, Shlomo, and Dina shared a bed, sleeping three across.

Despite the hardships, Dina tried to give her children some semblance of normalcy. Knowing how badly Rachel missed school and learning, Dina arranged for tutors to teach her geography, math, history, and religion.

One dark night in March 1942, the Germans quietly entered the ghetto and pounced on everyone they could find in the streets and alleys. The soldiers nabbed 65 Jews and spirited them away. About 5:00 a.m., residents heard gunfire coming from the sand pit outside the ghetto near

Borisov Street. At sunrise, they discovered 65 bodies lying in the pit.

In April, rumors spread that nearby towns east of Dokszyce were *Judenfrei*—free of all Jews. Days later, pro-Nazi police barged into the ghetto and arrested dozens of Jews on trumped-up charges. The next day, the police made a group of teenagers deepen the sand pit and then executed the arrested Jews.

The Nazis ratcheted up the terror level at the end of April. They announced there would be a mandatory *Appell* and that it was forbidden for anyone to leave the ghetto. Failure to show up was punishable by death. As she had done for previous *Appells*, Rachel hid with her mother and immediate family members at home in a secret place. Her grandfather had built it years earlier at the height of the Russian pogroms—organized massacres of a populace—against Jews between 1918 and 1920. He had constructed a false wall between the back of the house and an attached warehouse, creating a two-and-a-half-foot-wide space for the family to hide. He also carved out an underground bunker below the kitchen pantry, which had a trapdoor in the floor.

The day after the latest *Appell*—which counted 2,516 Jews—Germans and their henchmen entered the ghetto and began snatching hundreds of men, women, and children and marching them to a square in front of a destroyed synagogue. Those Jews who had work permits were sent home. The rest were murdered in a wholesale slaughter.

About a week later, Rachel and others were asleep when the Nazis pounded on the front door. She, Shlomo, and Dina grabbed some clothes and scrambled up the side of their brick bread oven to gain secret access to the attic. Then they crawled across the attic to an opening and went down a makeshift ladder into their hiding place between the two walls. They were joined by Rachel's maternal grandmother, Hinda Bayla, and two children who were members of a family living in the house. By this time, the Nazis had burst into the home and were grabbing all the others who hadn't fled in time.

"Be quiet," Dina whispered to the children. "Sit down and don't move. We're going to be here awhile."

The massacre dragged on for days because frustrated Nazis had to search in each building for the many Jews who, like the Mutterperls, had gone into hiding. Having run out of food and water, some Jews tried to escape and were captured and killed. Dina had the foresight to stock the hiding place with water, bread, and dried fruit. They used a bucket for a toilet. There was nothing Rachel could do except sit and hope the Nazis would give up looking for them before the supplies ran out.

After more than a week in hiding, Rachel and the others heard Nazis in the house, rummaging around and searching for the missing Jews. The intruders failed to find them.

Eventually, the house turned silent, and the gunfire and

shouting outside had all but ceased. Just when Rachel thought she would lose her mind if she had to stay hidden one more hour, Dina whispered, "I think it's okay to leave now." Quietly, they climbed the ladder to the attic. Not hearing anyone, they crossed to the other side and went down the secret access behind the stove.

To their dismay, they soon heard voices again in the house. "We must hide!" Dina whispered. There wasn't enough time to get up to the attic and into the hideaway. "Let's go to the bunker!"

As soldiers prowled around, Rachel and the others quietly scurried to the pantry in the back of the kitchen, lifted up the trapdoor, and jumped into the hidey-hole that had been dug under the floor. First went Shlomo, then Rachel, the two children, and Dina. The soldiers were now only a few feet from the kitchen. As the last person, Hinda realized there was no time for her to hide without giving away the bunker's location. She closed the trapdoor and covered it with a rug just as the soldiers entered the pantry.

One of them, an officer, gripped her roughly by the arm and demanded, "Tell me who else is with you."

Pretending to act like a senile old lady, Hinda widened her eyes to look deranged and replied, "I don't know. Am I supposed to be with someone?"

"Where did you come from?"

"I don't remember. Can you tell me where am I now?"

Angry and frustrated, the officer shoved her toward one of the soldiers and said, "She's crazy. Take her away. And keep searching the house."

They scoured each room but didn't find either hiding place. After the Germans left, the survivors crept out of the bunker. The house had been ransacked and looted of everything of value. Closets, shelves, and drawers had been stripped of their contents and rooms had been emptied. "We must leave the ghetto," Dina said.

Late that night, Dina gathered some hidden valuables to use in case she had to pay a ransom for their lives. Then she led Rachel, Shlomo, and the other two children out of the house. Scampering silently from one shadowed area to another, they headed toward the river. Bodies of the murdered still lay sprawled on the streets and sidewalks. Debris from broken windows and busted doors littered the ground. Torn shades and curtains fluttered in the breeze.

After reaching the river, they waded across a shallow area. The other side was farmland, where Dina hoped to find sanctuary with a family friend. As they climbed the riverbank, they were ambushed by two civilian militiamen who leveled rifles at them. "Halt!" ordered one of the men. "One more step and we'll shoot."

Rachel gulped and squeezed Dina's hand so tight her knuckles turned white. "Please, put your guns down," Dina begged. "I'm just trying to save these innocent children."

The men shook their heads and kept their weapons trained on her. She recognized them and they recognized her.

"Look, I can make you both rich," she said. "I have some valuables, some expensive jewelry. I'll give it all to you if you let us go."

The men looked at each other, nodded, and slung the rifles over their shoulders. They stuck their hands out, and Dina put the valuables in their palms. While the men ogled the jewelry, Dina and the children darted off into the darkness. Rachel and Shlomo followed their mother while the other two children ran in a different direction.

The trio dashed to the farmhouse of Beryl's best gentile friend, Wiktor Kosacki*. Rachel had fond memories of her family visiting Wiktor and his family two years earlier to celebrate Christmas and decorate their Christmas tree. Safely inside, Dina explained to Wiktor what had happened. Even though he knew it was dangerous, he agreed to hide Shlomo.

Then Dina and Rachel hid with Wiktor's sister Nadia*. Later, one of Wiktor's older sons showed up at Nadia's house and told Dina, "The Nazis came and beat up my father until he told them where Shlomo was hiding, and then they took the boy away. The Germans know you're alive and hiding somewhere around here. They're offering people 10 kilos [22 pounds] of sugar for pointing out any hidden Jews."

"You better run," Nadia told Dina. "There's a bathhouse in the next village that won't be used for a few days. Hide there."

After staying in the bathhouse, they moved at night and hid in fields during the day until they reached the house of Shlomo's nanny, Anna Dabrowski*. They couldn't stay long because they knew once the Nazis found out Anna was the boy's nanny, she would be suspected of harboring Dina and Rachel.

After asking Anna to get information about Shlomo, Dina took Rachel into a cornfield to hide. Later, Rachel was curled up out of view in the tall stalks when some peasants walked by. The girl didn't hear everything they said, but it was enough to shake her: "Isn't it good news? The Germans have cleaned out the town of all the Jews. It's *Judenfrei*."

Dina hoped she would be given the chance—however slim—to raise enough money to pay a ransom for Shlomo's release. The next day, Anna went into the cornfield and found Dina and Rachel. Breaking down in tears, Anna said, "Oh, Mrs. Mutterperl, it's so hard to say this, but Shlomo is dead. I went into Dokszyce, and the Nazis were only too glad to tell me that all the Jews they had gathered yesterday were lined up and shot. Shlomo was one of them."

The news was such a blow to Rachel that she barely heard anything else that Anna said. It was something about Wiktor getting into a bitter argument with his mother-in-law, who then informed the authorities that he was hiding a Jewish boy. The woman had given up the life of a child for 10 kilos of sugar.

It's just Mama and me from now on, Rachel thought. *But how long before they catch us?*

She made a mental note to remember the date of Shlomo's death—June 7, 1942. He was only six years old. Rachel saw a look of devastation in her mother, but it soon turned into a fierce determination that they wouldn't suffer a similar fate.

"We have to run, Rachel," Dina said. "We have to save ourselves."

After hiding in the fields for several days, they reached the farm of Germaine Zaloga*, a French-born widow whom Beryl had helped financially. Germaine wasn't home, but her teenage daughter, Carla*, was there and let them inside. Later, when Carla saw her mother returning with several peasant women, she ushered Rachel and Dina into a tiny hiding spot behind the fireplace. Germaine and her guests came into the house and carried on a lengthy conversation, unaware that just a few feet away were two hidden Jews on the run.

After the guests left, Rachel and Dina emerged from their hiding place and explained why they were there.

Germaine was sympathetic. "After my husband died, Mr. Mutterperl came to my aid and saved my farm when I thought my life was over," she told Dina. "I'll do anything to help you."

Referring to a nearby Polish town, Dina said, "We might be safer in the ghetto in Glebokie. I know a lot of people there."

"My son can take you in our horse and buggy," Germaine said. "But how will you get in there?"

"We will pose as gentiles and mingle with the crowd on market day," Dina said.

Rachel and Dina, wearing peasant clothes that Carla and Germaine had given them, arrived in Glebokie (now known as Glubokoye, Belarus) and slipped into the ghetto. They weren't aware that a few days earlier, on June 19, more than 2,500 Jews considered unfit for work had been taken out to the nearby Borek forest and killed.

Once inside the ghetto, Dina, who was 36, used her contacts to secure identification papers for the two of them. Rachel's ID had belonged to a 12-year-old girl, also named Rachel, who had been nabbed by the Nazis. Because the girl didn't have her papers with her, she had been taken away and murdered. Rachel's new documents made her older than her real age of nine, so she qualified for work at a fabric mill outside the ghetto. Her job was to tie thread whenever it broke on one of the spooling machines. Dina, meanwhile, did laundry and other household tasks for German officers.

The Nazis were methodically reducing the population of the ghetto through what they told the Jews were "resettlements" to work camps. In reality, the Jews were being sent to death camps.

A few months after arriving in Glebokie, Dina learned that some Jews planned to join the partisans who were living in the forests, conducting hit-and-run attacks against the Germans. Dina figured the ghetto would soon be liquidated and that the best chance for survival was for her and Rachel to become partisans. But there were several obstacles she would have to overcome. The partisans didn't want to accept anyone who brought children or didn't bring a weapon. Dina had a child and no weapon.

She contacted a gentile farmer who had been a friend of Beryl's. On market day, when farmers sold produce to Jews at the ghetto gates, he began providing extra food for Dina and Rachel. After Dina told him she wanted to join the partisans, he returned the following week on market day and handed her a basket of eggs that sat on a pile of straw. Under the straw was her "admission ticket" to the partisans—a gun, a German Luger apparently taken off a dead soldier.

A few days later, Dina and Rachel put on Germaine's and Carla's peasant clothes. Dina donned a babushka to conceal her jet-black hair and hid her gun in the bottom of a bag. The two went barefoot to make them look even more like peasants.

At the ghetto gate, they showed their work permits to the guards and walked out. After mixing in with non-Jews in the town, the pair ripped off their yellow badges and kept on walking. There was no turning back now. If they were caught, they were dead.

While the two were striding down a country road a few miles from town, seemingly out of nowhere a military truck pulled up beside them.

"Mama!" Rachel gasped under her breath. "Germans!"

"Don't panic," whispered Dina. "Just smile and be quiet. I'll handle this."

One of the soldiers in the cab asked, "Can we give you ladies a ride?"

Not wanting to draw any suspicion, she told them, "How thoughtful of you to offer. Of course, we'll accept." Rachel and Dina rode in the back of the truck and got off at the nearest village, making sure to avoid the town where the soldiers were headed.

The two continued on foot into the forest until they found a small band of partisans, who were not friendly. After Dina explained how she and her daughter had escaped from Glebokie and wanted to join them, one of the partisans growled, "A woman and a child are a burden. What benefit are you two to us?"

"My daughter and I can cook better than any of you," Dina answered. "We are brave. And I have a gun." After he scoffed at her, Dina said, "Well, we'll go someplace else where we're wanted."

The man lunged for her weapon. Dina stepped back, pointed it at him, and said, "I know how to shoot."

Just then, the leader of the group showed up. Dina once

again explained the reason for their presence. "We can be of great value to you," she told him. "We can cook and I can shoot and I know every square inch of this area."

The leader agreed to take Rachel and Dina into his 30-member group, which conducted reconnaissance missions for a much larger division operating deeper in the forest under the leadership of Russian officer Dmitry Medvedev. Members included Russian soldiers, farmers, peasants, and Jewish escapees who all shared a common enemy—the Nazis. The partisans specialized in sabotaging railway lines. They loosened bolts and unfastened the ties under train tracks at sharp curves to cause derailments of German troop and supply trains. They also disrupted German communication lines, blew up ammunition depots, and ambushed enemy patrols. It was a kill-or-be-killed existence.

Acting as her mother's assistant, Rachel helped prepare food and forage for nuts and berries. She also disassembled weapons and cleaned them because her little fingers could get into places that adult fingers couldn't. At times, she lugged heavy belts of ammunition.

Life was tough and primitive for Rachel and Dina. As partisans, they were constantly on the move, often camping out in the woods and marshes. Sometimes they slept in barns and, if they were really lucky, accepted a farmer's invitation to rest on the floor of his home. The houses in the forest had no running water, electricity, or bathrooms, but they were still a welcome relief from sleeping outdoors.

Rachel and Dina ate only after the partisans had eaten their meal, which was mostly potatoes, grain, onions, bread, and an occasional piece of meat. Whenever the pair had prepared pork for the partisans, Rachel and Dina wouldn't eat it, despite their hunger, because consuming pork was against their religion.

The winter was brutal, especially when food was scarce and shelter did little to protect them from the frigid winds and snow. The nights were unbearably cold, forcing mother and daughter to huddle together on piles of straw. Exposed to the teeth-chattering, bone-numbing low temperatures, Rachel suffered frostbite.

The partisans' daily battle to survive extended beyond dealing with the severe elements, lack of food, and flimsy shelter. Enemy troops were constantly on the hunt for them. So, too, were many peasants who tried to collect bounties for killing or capturing partisans.

A woman partisan in the group was caught by the Germans during a recon mission. They hacked her to death and stuffed her remains in a potato sack for her comrades to find. "The Nazis are sending us a message," said a partisan. "But we will not be intimidated. We will seek our revenge."

Rachel felt threatened every minute of every hour. She

never felt safe. No matter where she was or what she was doing, she was always on guard. Every night, she felt relieved she had made it through another difficult, anxiety-ridden day. Sleep came from exhaustion, not from any peace of mind.

Rachel accepted that her odds of survival were slim. She believed if she did come out of the forest alive at war's end, it would be because she had put all her faith and trust in her mother. Whatever Dina told her to do, she did without question because, up to now, they were still alive when so many other Jews were dead.

In early 1943, the Soviet Union began sending small planes that landed on an ice-covered lake to deliver arms and medical supplies to bolster the partisans, who had evolved from a mere annoyance to a serious threat to German troops in eastern Europe. The partisans had burned down much of the center of Nazi-controlled Dokszyce.

Near the end of the year, Rachel contracted typhus and was transported in a sleigh to the infirmary at the unit's headquarters. For weeks, she battled the deadly disease. Eventually, her high fever broke, but she was still too weak to walk and could barely stand up on her own.

During Rachel's slow recovery, the Germans launched a last-ditch operation to surround the partisans in the forests and wipe them out for good. As this ominous shrinking blockade got under way in spring 1944, the partisans scattered and tried to blend in with the peasants. Because the Germans weren't sure who was and wasn't a partisan or a partisan sympathizer, they were rounding up everyone they encountered—farmers, peasants, villagers—and interrogating them.

Rachel, who was still recovering from her bout with typhus, and Dina went out on their own together. "Be careful and don't talk too much," Dina told Rachel, who was wearing pants and had her head shaved to prevent lice.

As they hiked through the forest, Rachel, now 11, somehow lost sight of her mother. She called out but was afraid to yell too loudly for fear of attracting the attention of German troops who were stalking the woods. Fighting off the urge to panic, the girl searched for her mother but couldn't find her anywhere.

Weary and frightened and hungry, Rachel caved in to her fears and lost her will to live. *I can't find Mama. I'm lost, alone, and I don't know how I can survive by myself. If the Germans catch me, they're going to kill me anyway. They kill all Jews. So why suffer any longer? I might as well let the Germans shoot me now.*

She emerged from the woods and reached a wide clearing. From the other side, German troops began firing at her. As bullets slammed into the ground in front of her, Rachel stood still, waiting for one to strike her dead.

Suddenly, she heard a voice calling, "Rachel! Rachel!" *It's Mama!* The girl wheeled around and sprinted back into the woods and into her mother's arms.

"I've been searching for you," said Dina, holding her tightly. "I heard the gunfire, and I was so afraid they had shot you."

The warm feeling Rachel felt in her mother's embrace didn't last long because they had to keep moving. As refugees, they roamed the area in search of food and shelter until they were caught in a German roundup of peasants and farmers and brought to Dokszyce for questioning. Those suspected of being partisans or their sympathizers were hanged on a makeshift gallows.

Meanwhile, Rachel, Dina, and the other captives were held in a big warehouse. Afraid someone would recognize her, Dina pretended to be sick and hid her face, pulling her babushka low over her forehead. It was mostly up to Rachel to find food for them. Because children were allowed outside, she went into the streets and begged.

The guards noticed Rachel was in boys' clothes and sporting fuzz for hair. They began to debate whether she was a boy or a girl. Because she spoke Yiddish—a language similar to German—she could make out what the soldiers were saying in German: "He's a boy. Look at the way he's dressed. And he doesn't have hair." "She's a girl. You can tell by her face."

The Germans then announced women would go free, but men would be put into forced labor. Fearing the soldiers thought she was a boy, Rachel shouted in German, *"Mädchen! Mädchen!"* ("Girl! Girl!")

"You know German?" an officer asked Rachel. His face twisted in fury and he hissed, "Then you must be a Jew!" Turning to the guards, he ordered, "Hang her."

So scared she couldn't speak, Rachel was led to the gallows. Above her swayed two nooses strung to a thick branch that rested between two poles.

After being alerted by a fellow captive that Rachel was about to be hanged, Dina rushed out of the warehouse toward the gallows, shouting, "Don't kill her! She's my daughter!"

"If she's your daughter, then you must be a Jew as well," snarled the officer, his ice-cold eyes boring into her.

"I am not Jewish and neither is my daughter," claimed Dina, who was going to do whatever it took—even deny her own faith—to save Rachel.

"If she isn't your daughter, then you must have been hiding this Jew. She knows German, and she's trying to pass herself off as a boy."

"She lost her hair when she was sick from typhus, and she's wearing boys' clothes because she has nothing else to wear," explained Dina in a quivering voice. "She's picked up a few common German words because she helps me do laundry for Germans like you."

The officer turned to Rachel and asked her the meaning of several German words such as *Brot* (bread) and *Wasser* (water). Afraid to say too much, she gave the meaning of some words but pretended not to know others.

The officer wasn't convinced. Turning to Dina, he said, "You have been harboring this Jewish child and she must hang. Tell me the truth and I will spare your life. Admit she's Jewish."

"No! No! No!" Dina cried.

"You're lying!"

Near hysterics, Dina shrieked in a rising voice, "I have worked for you Germans. I have done your laundry and been devoted to the Nazi cause. And now you want to hang my child? She is my only daughter and I don't want her to die alone, so hang me. I beg of you, kill me first because I can't bear to see my child die." Wagging her finger at the officer, she lied, "Just know you will be killing two gentiles and not two Jews because we . . . are . . . not . . . Jewish!"

Terror had frozen all thoughts from Rachel's mind. She stood rooted below the nooses, shaking uncontrollably while the officer discussed with his comrades whether she should live or die.

When they finally reached agreement, the officer strolled over to Dina and Rachel and said, "You are free to go."

Having been so close to death, Rachel took a few seconds to get her mind and body functioning again. It was as if all blood had been drained from her veins and she needed time for it to start flowing. Having withstood this latest peril, she wondered, *How much more of this can I survive?*

The pair tried to find a place where they could fit in. But

anti-Semitism was so rampant that, to Rachel, every peasant, every farmer, every gentile in every village they entered was their potential murderer. Because Dina was well known, she had to remain relatively hidden, leaving it to Rachel to continue begging and gleaning the fields for food.

At one village, a woman approached Dina and said, "I know who you are, but I won't turn you in. I came to warn you. I overheard someone talk about you and say, 'She thinks nobody knows who she is.' You'd better leave before she informs the militia that you are Jewish."

Rachel and Dina fled the village and joined another partisan group, remaining with it until the area was liberated by the Red Army in summer 1944. Then they returned to Dokszyce, where Dina dug up the valuables and money she had buried years earlier.

While Dina was home, Mrs. Malinowski*, a neighbor who was a gentile, came over and handed her a crumpled photo of Rachel, Shlomo, and Dina. "I found it in the trash after the liquidation and I saved it, hoping you would return so I could give it to you," said Mrs. Malinowski. "You were always good to me." In Dina's heart, the photo was more valuable than any piece of jewelry because it was the only picture she had of the three of them.

"I must tell you something," Mrs. Malinowski added. "Your life is in danger. There's a rumor going around that people are plotting to kill you. Leave as soon as you can." She provided Dina and Rachel with some food before the pair left Dokszyce for good.

Needing to flee their homeland, Dina hired a guide in Lublin, Poland, to help them get to a displaced persons camp in Italy, more than 1,300 miles (2,092 kilometers) away. After several grueling months of dangerous travel and hiking over the imposing Alps, Rachel and her mother—their clothes tattered, their bodies worn out, their stomachs empty—reached the Italian border.

As she crossed into Italy, Rachel saw something waving in the breeze that brought her the sense of peace and joy missing from her life for so many years. It was blue and white and emblazoned with the Star of David—the flag flown by the Jewish Brigade, a military unit of handpicked Jewish soldiers. They were under the command of the British Army, which occupied that part of Italy. Rachel smiled at her mother and said, "I finally feel safe."

In 1947, Rachel and Dina emigrated to the United States with sponsorship and support from Beryl's sister in Brooklyn. While attending school, Rachel had a part-time job painting piggy banks and figurines for 50 cents an hour. In 1952, she became an American citizen and married Harvey Goldfarb, a Holocaust survivor who served in the Korean War. Together, they raised two children and have two grandchildren. Rachel was a real estate agent for 30 years in the Washington, DC, area before retiring in

1982. She has been a longtime volunteer at the United States Holocaust Memorial Museum.

Dina, who worked in sales, never remarried. In 2006, at the age of 99, she died on June 7—the same date of death as her son, Shlomo.

Rachel, known by friends and acquaintances as Rae, says she has a simple message for students: "Love your family, appreciate the freedom this country has given you, and practice tolerance."

This story is based on Rachel's interview, Dina's recollections as told to Rachel, and the written accounts of Holocaust survivors of Dokszyce.

THE WAR NAME

FRITZ FRIEDMANN

(Fred Friedman)

❦

Six-year-old Fritz Friedmann was walking along a busy sidewalk in Vienna, Austria, with his father, Hugo, toward an ice-cream shop. Suddenly, several trucks squealed around the corner and screeched to a stop. A few dozen fierce-looking thugs—each clad in a brown shirt with a leather strap across the chest, riding pants, and boots—streamed out of the vehicles.

"It's the SA," Hugo gasped. Members of the SA, short for *Sturmabteilung* (German for "Assault Division"), were also known as Brownshirts, the storm troopers who comprised the paramilitary wing of the Nazi party.

Spreading out on both sides of the street, the Brownshirts shouted to the frightened pedestrians, "Show us your papers!" The storm troopers began shoving men to one side of the street and women to the other.

Hugo, a tall, lanky, mild-mannered man with a kind heart

and gentle soul, trembled as he handed his identity papers over to the six Brownshirts who surrounded him. When they saw he was Jewish, they roughed him up and yanked him toward the other side of the street. Hugo kept falling down, and every time he did, they kicked him.

Never seeing such violence before, little Fritz cried out, "Stop! Stop hurting my papa!" Bursting into tears, the distraught boy followed them, shouting, "Leave my papa alone!" Annoyed by the child's plea, one of the Brownshirts wheeled around, grabbed Fritz by the arm, and threw him down.

When the attacks stopped, about a dozen Jewish men were forced to draw large swastikas on the street with chalk. The Jewish women, who also had been detained, were then ordered to get on their hands and knees and scrub the swastikas off with brushes and buckets of water. When the women finished, the men were made to draw new swastikas, which were again removed, under duress, by the women. After the harassment ended, the women were released, but the men, including Hugo, were tossed into the back of a truck and whisked away.

Reeling in shock and fear, Fritz stood alone on the sidewalk, weeping uncontrollably.

This was the new life faced by Jews in Vienna beginning in March 1938 after Germany took over control of Austria. The

Nazi propaganda machine called the occupation the *Anschluss*, or annexation of the country. But it was really a bloodless invasion.

Like so many kids in Vienna at the time, Fritz came from a family coping with the country's shaky economy. His parents, Hugo and Adela, ran a knitting business out of their modest apartment. Using two large cast-iron, hand-powered knitting machines and a heavy spooling machine, the couple toiled 10 to 12 hours a day, turning out sweaters, shawls, and clothes for major department stores and area shops.

The couple often took Fritz to the Prater, a large public park that featured amusement rides, including one of Europe's tallest Ferris wheels. They couldn't afford to buy rides for Fritz, but that was okay with him. He enjoyed just being there with his parents and soaking up the park's positive energy.

The boy looked forward to Friday night dinners, when the apartment was filled with extended family members savoring chicken soup and gefilte fish. Even though the apartment had only one bedroom, aunts, uncles, and cousins often spent the night sleeping on the floor.

For Fritz, most every day was a good day. But the good times faded after the *Anschluss*.

And now he was alone, sobbing hysterically on the sidewalk, having just witnessed Brownshirts attacking and kidnapping his father.

A gentile woman who watched the assaults hurried over to the traumatized boy and calmed him down. "Where do you live?" she asked.

His chest still heaving from crying so hard, he replied, "22 Spaungasse."

She took him by the hand, walked him to his apartment, and explained to Adela what had happened. Listening to the disturbing details, Adela was horrified but also furious. After the other woman left, Adela told Fritz, "I must find your papa." Although she was petite—she stood only four feet nine inches tall—Adela possessed a giant-size reserve of courage and determination. "Fritzie, you stay here and don't answer the door for anyone," she said on her way out.

Once again, the boy found himself alone. Even though he was only six, he was aware how dangerous the Nazis and their sympathizers were to Jews, and he fretted over his father's fate. As time dragged on, his anxiety heightened.

Finally, the door opened. Fritz looked up and shouted, "Papa! Mama!" He rushed into the arms of his father, who scooped him up and hugged and kissed him. "I was so worried about you!" Fritz said.

"I'm here now, Fritzie, and I'm fine," Hugo replied, forcing a smile.

Fritz noticed that his father's appearance had changed dramatically. From the smiling, sparkly-eyed dad of a few hours ago, Hugo had turned into a pale, gaunt, dejected man.

Trying to reassure Fritz, Hugo said, "Everything is going to be okay."

But it wasn't okay. Nothing was okay anymore since the Nazi occupation. In Fritz's mind, it seemed the whole world had turned against the Jews. As the only Jewish boy in his first-grade class, Fritz became targeted for abuse. Classmates began bullying him, fighting him, and calling him "dirty Jew" and "Jew dog" until his parents pulled him out of school.

Catholic neighbors in the next apartment, whom the Friedmanns considered close friends, refused to speak to them anymore and wouldn't allow their son Heinz to play with Fritz, even though the two had been good pals. To further display their anti-Semitism, Heinz and his dad began wearing Brownshirt-like uniforms.

The Friedmanns later learned that Hugo was the only person released among those nabbed on the street that awful day. Some of the victims—including a good family friend—were sent directly to Dachau, Germany, site of the Nazis' first major concentration camp.

More than 76,000 people—mostly Jews—were arrested in the first few weeks after the *Anschluss*. Universities banned Jews, emptying campuses of more than 40 percent of their students and professors. Many Jews' property was confiscated and their homes looted by Nazi officials.

Hugo and Adela seldom went outside their apartment, and when they did, it was only for necessities. They often walked no farther than across the street to the Jewish-owned grocery store, until the Nazis closed it down.

Later that summer, Fritz and his parents were listening to the radio when they heard pounding on their apartment door and shouts of, "Gestapo! Open up!" Hugo opened it and two officers and two soldiers stormed in. "You have four hours to vacate this place," one of the officers barked. "If you are still here when we return, you will be arrested." Seeing these mean men yelling at his father nearly paralyzed Fritz, triggering images of the street attack.

When the Gestapo left, Adela broke down and wept, causing Fritz to cry, too. He knew his mom was the tough one in the family. She had gone through World War I as a child. After her father died, she had helped her mother take care of her four siblings and held down a job stuffing tobacco into cigarettes. Three generations of Adela's family had lived in this fifth-floor walk-up apartment, and now she, Hugo, and Fritz had only a few hours to gather their things and move out.

After her crying jag ended, Adela wiped away the tears and took charge. She and Hugo decided to move into the one-room apartment above the carriage house behind the apartment building. Working at a furious pace, they dismantled the heavy knitting machinery and hauled it down into the tiny space, which had a coal stove but no running water or bathroom. Fritz and his parents hustled down and up five flights until they transferred everything to the carriage house apartment before the deadline.

Life became increasingly perilous for the Jews of Vienna. Friends and relatives were beaten up, arrested, released, and then beaten up again. Despite the dangers, Hugo and Adela let Fritz walk to the park alone because he had blondish hair and didn't look Jewish. "It sometimes is better if you go to the park," his mother explained. "But when you come back, first look at the door and see if the Gestapo or the German police are here. If they are, then don't come in."

On the nights of November 9 and 10, 1938, a wave of violent attacks against Jews by storm troopers and members of Hitler Youth organizations swept through Germany, Austria, and a section of Czechoslovakia known as the Sudetenland.

From their vantage point, the Friedmanns could hear anti-Semitic mobs roaming the streets, smashing the windows of Jewish-owned stores, and assaulting Jews in their homes, businesses, community centers, and places of worship. In Vienna alone, more than 40 synagogues were burned, 4,000 Jewish shops were vandalized and looted, and Jewish cemeteries were desecrated. Throughout the Nazi-controlled regions, rioters destroyed 267 synagogues, more than 7,500 Jewish-owned commercial establishments, and murdered at least 90 Jews. The violence, which was orchestrated by the Nazis, became known as *Kristallnacht* (German for "Night of

Crystal"). It was named after the tons of shattered glass that littered the streets.

The Friedmanns had seen enough; they made it their ultimate goal to reach England by going through Germany and into Belgium, where they hoped to board a ship. They obtained papers stamped with a swastika that authorized them to leave Austria. In January 1939, carrying what little they could, they headed to the train station.

The Friedmanns arrived in Cologne, Germany, where they stayed for several weeks with a Jewish family. Three times the Friedmanns tried to cross into Belgium, but German guards repeatedly turned them back. Eventually, the Jewish underground put the family in touch with a Jewish barber in Belgium who rented them his passport, which allowed them into the country.

The Friedmanns lived with the barber, his wife, and eight children in a cramped, noisy, two-bedroom apartment in Antwerp. While Hugo and Adela worked as knitters, Fritz went to school and sharpened his language skills by learning Dutch and German. He was feeling like a normal kid again.

But on May 10, 1940, Germany invaded Belgium, and less than three weeks later, Belgium surrendered. Once again, the Friedmanns found themselves under Nazi oppression.

Trying to flee to England, they pushed their way onto a train heading for the coast. But because the Germans were bombing the rails, it was impossible for the train to reach its destination, so all the passengers had to get off.

Joining an endless stream of hundreds of thousands of refugees, the Friedmanns wandered from village to village, sleeping in barns, in fields, and in forests while often diving for cover from strafing German planes. As the family kept walking toward the coast, Fritz passed old people too weary to move, bodies of victims who had been strafed, and smoldering military trucks that had been bombed.

The Friedmanns' hopes of reaching England crumbled when they discovered that German troops stood between them and the coast. With little options left after two months on the road as refugees, the family gave up. Hitching rides on the back of farm wagons—including one carrying manure— they returned to Antwerp.

They moved to the larger city of Brussels in summer 1941, hoping it would be easier to hide from the Nazis. The family settled on another five-story walk-up apartment, this one at 28 Rue du Foyer Schaerbeekois.

A few months later, in the fall, Adela sat Fritz down and said, "You know what's going on with the Nazis, right?" Seeing him nod, she continued. "It's getting much too dangerous here, Fritzie. Papa and I have decided you belong somewhere safer. Here is what will happen: Tomorrow morning I will take you to the train station and then someone will take you to a safe place without us."

Adela was blunt and to the point and kept the conversation short. Fritz could see in her eyes and hear in her voice that her heart was breaking. Hugo didn't say anything because it was simply too emotionally difficult for him to talk about sending his only child away. Fritz, who was now nine, didn't protest. *They're just trying to protect me*, he thought. *All this terrible stuff will stop soon, and I'll be back home*. At least that's what he hoped would happen.

The next morning, Adela accompanied him to the train station, where he joined five other Jewish children who were going to the same place. They were met by Andrée Geulen, a brave 20-year-old teacher who was a Christian secretly working with the Jewish Defense Committee escorting Jewish children to safe havens. Pretty and short, Andrée spoke softly with a mix of warmth and confidence that eased some of the apprehension that Fritz and the other kids felt.

"I'm going to take you to a place that will be like a little vacation where you'll play with other children and eat good food and, most importantly of all, be safe," she said. "On the train, all of you will behave nicely and not talk to anybody."

She brought the group to a majestic chateau that had been converted into an orphanage in the village of Jamoigne-sur-Semois near the French border about 110 miles (177 kilometers) from Brussels. To the general public, the chateau housed orphans of Belgian soldiers. But secretly, it also hid Jewish children, who made up nearly half the number of residents. The home's manager, Marie Taquet-Martens, took care of the kids' daily needs while her husband, Emile Taquet, a Belgian officer, handled administrative matters.

The children slept on foldable cots in the spacious main foyer of the chateau. Although the setting was beautiful, Fritz disliked the stern staff and the regimented life of the orphanage. Besides, he was homesick. About two weeks after his arrival, he made up his mind: *I can't stay here. I'm going to run away and go back home.*

In the middle of the night, the boy sneaked out of the chateau and trekked about three miles (five kilometers) to the train station. Even though he had no money, he boarded the first train that arrived in the morning. He didn't know where it was headed, but luck was on his side, because it was going to Brussels. Without thinking it through, he locked himself in the bathroom. After the train got under way, the conductor knocked on the bathroom door and said, "I know you're in there. Come out now."

Fritz obediently opened the door. When the conductor asked if he had a ticket or money for one, the boy shook his head no. The conductor rolled his eyes, pointed to a nearby seat, and said, "Go sit there and don't talk to anyone."

Doing what he was told, Fritz arrived safely in Brussels and walked home. When he appeared out of the blue, his mother didn't know whether to embrace him or scold him. She did both. After hugging and kissing him, she laced into him. "Are you absolutely crazy?" she howled. "Are you out of your mind? Do you know what you did? You put yourself at great risk. What am I going to do with you now to keep you safe?"

Like Adela, Hugo was torn over his son's return—thrilled to see him again but concerned over the boy's safety because of the Nazis' stepped-up efforts to clear the city of Jews. So many friends and relatives had been taken away already.

Shortly after Fritz had returned to Brussels, he went to play at Parc Josaphat, a large park near his home. Soon, Louise Beauclaire, a cute 12-year-old girl he liked but would never tell her so, came over to him.

"You can't go back to your apartment," said Louise, the daughter of a Catholic who owned a grocery store across the street from where the Friedmanns lived. "The Gestapo is in your building. Stay in the park and I will get you when it's safe."

Fritz's nerves were on edge as he waited and worried for word about his parents. Three hours later, Louise showed up. "Your mother and father are with my parents," she told him. "I'll take you to them." Seeing the relief on his face, she said, "Walk behind me, but not too close. I can't be seen with you because, well, you're . . ."

"Jewish," he said, finishing her sentence. He understood that if Louise were suspected of helping him, or any Jew, her life would be in jeopardy.

"When I go into my parents' store, wait a minute and then come in," she said.

A short while later, he entered the shop and was led to a small room in the back where his parents were hiding. "I was so afraid the Gestapo had taken you away," he said, hugging them.

"The Gestapo came for the Blums," his mother said, referring to the Jewish family who lived on the third floor. "Then the Gestapo knocked on our door, but we didn't answer it. We heard them rattling the knob, but the door was locked. One of them said, 'Nobody is home. The truck is already fully loaded [with Jews], so let's come back later.' We peeked out the window and when we saw the Gestapo leave, we ran over here without taking anything. Mr. Beauclaire has agreed to hide us until he finds us a different apartment."

A few days later, the store owner announced that he had secured for them another five-story walk-up apartment less than two blocks away on the same street, at 90 Rue du Foyer Schaerbeekois. That night, he walked the Friedmanns over to their new unfurnished residence.

The next day, Adela boldly went to their former place, No. 28, hurriedly packed some clothing in two suitcases, and scurried back to No. 90. She emptied the suitcases and planned to go back for another load. But, she complained to Fritz, "I am so tired."

"I'll go," he volunteered. "I can do this." He walked to

No. 28 and locked the door. While filling the suitcases, he heard a commotion downstairs. Gazing out the window carefully, so he wouldn't be spotted, he saw that the Gestapo had returned and brought movers with them. They began taking out furniture and accessories from the Blums' apartment.

What should I do? he asked himself. *Do I stay here and wait until they leave? But Mama heard them say they would be coming back to our apartment. What if they break down the door? They'll catch me. I better try to escape.*

After quickly finishing packing the suitcases, he tiptoed down the stairs. When he reached the landing of the third floor, he noticed the movers were maneuvering an armoire through the doorway of the apartment, blocking the view of the officers. *This is my chance.* As he scrambled down the stairs, he heard someone yell, "Halt! Halt!"

With a suitcase in each hand, Fritz dashed outside and sprinted faster than he ever had in his life. Afraid to look back because that would slow him down, he kept running until he reached No. 90 and bounded up the stairs to the apartment.

Seeing her son out of breath and looking terrified, she asked, "Fritzie, what happened to you?" After he told her, she let out a loud moan and said, "Why didn't you just drop the bags? There's nothing in them worth risking your life over. Oh, what I am going to do with you?"

At that moment, she knew exactly what she was going to do. Even though she put herself in danger by being seen in public, she made contact with Andrée again in January 1942 and asked her to find another safe place for Fritz. At first, Andrée declined because he had previously run away. But few people had a will stronger than the persistent Adela Friedmann. She badgered Andrée until the teacher reluctantly agreed to escort Fritz a second time.

Back home, Adela took him by the hand and said, "We're sending you off again. But this time you won't run away. Is that understood?"

"Yes, Mama."

Adela packed his bag and brought him to Andrée, who gave him a stern lecture: "What you did when you ran away was wrong. If you had been caught by the Nazis, they would have tortured you into telling them where the other children were. You were reckless and put them—and all of us—in danger. This is the last time I will help you, Fritz. You must promise me you will not run away again."

"I swear to you I won't."

"Okay, then," she said, giving him a hug. "You no longer are Fritz Friedmann." She handed him a set of false identity papers. "You have a new war name. From now on, you are Alfred DeWilde."

A train took them to the town of Bastogne, about 90 miles (145 kilometers) southeast of Brussels, close to the German border, where a Catholic seminary was caring for several hundred boys, many planning to become priests. Among them, however, were several dozen Jews who didn't reveal their true identities.

At the seminary, each kid slept in an individual alcove that had a bed, a wardrobe, and a large crucifix on the wall. Every weekday, Fritz and the others woke up at 5:00 a.m., attended Mass, did daily exercises in the courtyard, and then took a cold shower. There was no hot water. After breakfast came classroom studies, including plenty of religion, and then a break for lunch followed by class, more religious training, and dinner. Each table at mealtime held a dozen boys and a priest. Although Fritz wasn't pleased by the regimentation, he enjoyed the food.

Being raised Jewish, Fritz had to learn quickly what all the Catholic children had practiced for years. Because Mass was celebrated in Latin—a language he had never heard before—he had to pretend to speak it during worshippers' responses to the priest. He also had to copy a gesture that was strange to him—the right hand to the forehead, then to the abdomen, and finally to the left and right shoulders. He had no idea they were doing the sign of the cross. During his first Mass, he went up to the altar with the others and, following what they were doing, stuck out his tongue and let the priest place a small communion wafer on it. Not seeing anyone chew it, he let it dissolve in his mouth.

No one told him what to do during confession. When it was his turn to go into the darkened confessional booth, he saw the outline of the priest through a latticed opening. Fritz didn't know what to say, so he waited for the priest to ask him questions about any sins he had committed in the past week: Did you take anything that wasn't yours? Did you tell any lies? Did you use the Lord's name in vain? Did you have any impure thoughts?

Fritz didn't want to be labeled a problem child, so he said no to every question.

Convinced the boy wasn't willing to admit to anything, the priest said, "Let's do penance anyway. Say with me three Hail Marys and four Our Fathers."

Uh-oh, I'm in real trouble now, thought Fritz. He hadn't learned the prayers yet. *What should I do?* He began to mumble nonsense, hoping the priest wouldn't listen too carefully.

"Speak up, lad, speak up," said the priest.

"I am," Fritz replied. He then continued to mumble.

Realizing that it was crucial for his survival to act like a Catholic, Fritz learned the prayers and church rituals within a few days.

No one other than a few members of the seminary was supposed to know there were Jews among the students. Being curious and wanting to connect with fellow Jews, Fritz would go up to a boy he thought might be a hidden Jew and whisper a word in Yiddish. If the kid responded in Yiddish, then Fritz knew he was Jewish. If the boy said, "What did you say?"

Fritz replied, "Oh, nothing." Using this approach, he was able to make friends with several hidden Jews.

In August 1942, after more than eight months there, Fritz was unexpectedly hustled away along with about 10 other boys after priests learned the Gestapo was getting increasingly suspicious that the seminary was sheltering Jewish children. For the next four weeks, the boys were shuttled from one sanctuary to another, including a sanitarium and the basement of a hotel where Nazi officers often stayed.

During this period, the Germans were deporting Jews in Belgium to former military barracks in the city of Malines (known as Mechelen today), which was a transit camp that sent victims on to concentration camps. (From 1942 to 1944, 28 long trains would carry more than 25,000 Jews from Malines to Auschwitz-Birkenau, where they were exterminated.)

Meanwhile, Fritz ended up at an orphanage south of Brussels in the town of Cul-des-Sarts in September 1942. The orphanage—which held about 60 boys and girls, many of them hidden Jews—was in the sprawling Chateau Philippe, the former residence of a wealthy businessman. The girls were in one dormitory and the boys in another.

Run by the director, Madame Helene Van Hal, the orphanage rationed food, soap, shoes, and clothing. All the meals were the same. Breakfast was four slices of dark bread, jam or jelly, and a bowl of "baptized milk," the name the kids gave their watered-down milk. Lunch and dinner consisted mostly of mashed potatoes with cooked greens or mashed pea flakes.

School-age children attended one of two classrooms, where teachers taught combined grades. Because Fritz was the only fifth grader, he considered himself number one in his class. After their studies and chores, the boys and girls socialized and sometimes held dances in the chateau.

Shortly after Fritz's arrival at Cul-des-Sarts, Madame Van Hal was tipped off by the Belgian underground that the *Feldgendarmerie* (German military police) was coming to inspect the orphanage. Van Hal sprang into action. When all the children were assembled in the dining room, she carefully studied each one to determine who looked the most Jewish. Those who did were ordered to run and hide in the nearby woods until it was safe to return. She couldn't send out every Jew because that would raise suspicions about the whereabouts of so many missing children.

Fritz didn't have the typical Jewish features, so he was among those who stayed. Madame told him, "When the *Feldgendarmerie* come, they are going to question you to see if you are Jewish. Here's what you tell them: 'My mother is dead. My father works in Germany, but I don't know the city. He's working for the German army.' That is your story."

After the military police arrived, a stern-looking officer lined up the children and then, walking down the line, asked each one several questions. Fritz could feel his heart pounding as the officer moved toward him. *Stay calm. Breathe. Act confident.*

When the officer finally reached Fritz, the man asked, "What is your name?"

"Alfred DeWilde," Fritz lied, looking directly into his eyes.

"Where are you from, Alfred?"

"Antwerp, sir." *My mouth is so dry. Don't gulp.*

"Where are your parents?"

"My mother is dead and my father works for the German army, but I don't know the city." *He's staring at me. Does he not believe me?*

"How long have you been here?"

"One month, sir." *What if he suspects something? What if he . . .*

"Where were you before?"

"A seminary in Bastogne, sir." *Look at him like you have nothing to fear.*

"Why were you sent there?"

Uh-oh. Think! Think fast! "My father wanted me to become a priest." Seeing the officer staring quizzically at him, Fritz thought, *He's looking like he doesn't believe me. What if he pulls me out of line? Well, I won't let them take me alive . . .*

For several seconds, the officer studied him. Just when Fritz felt as though the built-up tension would buckle his knees, the officer moved on to the next child in line.

Fritz would have to endure four more unscheduled visits

and intimidating questions, sometimes from the Gestapo. Each time, he handled the nerve-racking ordeal with just enough poise to avoid any suspicions.

By summer, the children began seeing signs of a German retreat. Military vehicles, tanks, trucks, and troops rumbled past the orphanage. Then came the day that so many Belgians in the area waited for—their liberation. On an afternoon late in August 1944, a US Army jeep carrying three American soldiers arrived and was immediately surrounded by cheering villagers, who showered the GIs with flowers and kisses and gave them bottles of wine. After taking the bullets out of their pistols, the soldiers handed their guns and helmets to Fritz and the boys to play with. The GIs even posed for photos with the kids. For one picture, a smiling Fritz held up a .45 caliber pistol with a group of his pals.

Fritz, who was now 12, hadn't felt this happy since before the *Anschluss*. Over the next few days, American soldiers who were Jewish made extra trips to the orphanage to deliver chocolate and other goodies after learning many children there were Jews.

One of the GIs brought a guitar to the orphanage and tried to teach Fritz and a few other children a song called "South of the Border," a popular tune at the time. Among the first English words that Fritz learned was "South of the border, down Mexico way, that's where I fell in love when the stars above came out to play."

The boy didn't understand the meaning of the words. But so what? The song would forever be a reminder of the day Fritz Friedmann was liberated and no longer a hidden child.

In early September 1944, some parents, relatives, and family friends arrived at the orphanage to claim their children. By the end of October, Fritz and two other boys were the only ones left. "I was almost certain that my parents had been killed," he recalls. "But then my father showed up. I barely recognized him. He looked terrible—shrunken, thin, emaciated, and white as a sheet because he hadn't seen the sunlight for two and a half years. He had remained hidden in the apartment all that time."

Hugo escorted Fritz back to Brussels, where the boy returned to school and not only caught up with his studies but excelled in them and entered college at age 16. "It was weird getting my name back," he recalls. "When people asked me my name, I often said 'Alfred DeWilde' and then had to correct myself. I hadn't called myself Fritz Friedmann for so long that when I said it, it sounded as if I was talking about someone else.

"My friend Louise told me, 'In Belgium, we have a bad taste in our mouths about anything German. Fritz is a German name. From now on, I'm going to call you Freddy.' I've been Freddy ever since."

In 1949, the Friedmanns—Hugo, Adela, Freddy, and his baby brother, John, who was born after the war—emigrated to Israel. Drafted into the Israeli Air Force, Freddy became an electronics engineer specializing in navigation.

Five years later, he emigrated alone to the United States and became an American citizen, changing his name to Fred Fritz Friedman, dropping the last "n" of his family name. As a married man with two children, he worked as a computer design engineer in New York, New Jersey, Florida, and Europe. After Hugo passed away at age 41, Fred brought his mother and brother to the United States to live.

In 1989, Andrée Geulen was honored by Yad Vashem—Israel's Holocaust memorial—with the title Righteous Among the Nations for risking her life to help more than 300 Jewish children hide from the Nazis in Belgium during the war. At an emotional ceremony in 2007, Israel granted the then 86-year-old woman honorary citizenship and reunited her with dozens of the former child survivors she had saved.

Over the years, Fred has attended reunions or stayed in contact with some of his fellow hidden children. Retired and living in Miami, Florida, Fred, who has three grandchildren, continues to speak at schools, synagogues, and organizations.

"One thing has always stuck with me through all these years—never be a bystander when you see injustice," says Fred. "The bystanders who didn't speak out against the Nazis allowed anti-Semitism to fester and grow into the Holocaust. The ones who said nothing must share the blame. When you see injustice, you cannot turn away, because if you do, then you, too, are guilty of injustice. When you encounter bullying or intolerance or prejudice, it's your duty to speak out."

THE LOST TEARS

IREN FOGEL

(Irene Weiss)

For nine-year-old Iren Fogel, it was a scary feeling knowing she and her loved ones were hated not for anything they had done wrong but solely because they were Jewish.

As Orthodox Jews in Czechoslovakia, her family was feeling the sting of anti-Semitism after the region of their homeland where they lived fell under the control of Hungary's pro-Nazi government in 1939. At the time, Iren and sisters Szeren, 12, and Edit, 7, brothers Moshe, 11, Reuven, 4, and Gershon, 3, and parents Meyer and Leah, comprised one of 10 Jewish families in the small, relatively poor town of Botragy (population of 1,000).

New laws designed to oppress Jews went into effect, and over time became even harsher and more restrictive. Meyer's successful lumberyard was confiscated and given to a non-Jew without any compensation to the Fogels. Iren, Szeren, Moshe, and all young Jews were thrown out of public schools.

Because Jews had to identify themselves by wearing the yellow Star of David, they became targets of abuse. Roving bands of Nazi-inspired thugs beat them up on the street without fear of arrest because Jews had lost their civil rights. For her protection, Iren didn't stray far from home—a home she was grateful to still have. She sensed her parents' feelings of helplessness and vulnerability, which was frightening because if they didn't have the power to protect the family, who did? She knew the answer: no one.

Even though the Fogels had no income, they managed to survive during these trying times. They owned farmland and were able to grow their own food, some of which they exchanged for products and services.

In April 1944, the Nazis embarked on a cold-blooded agenda to rid Hungary of its 440,000 Jews. In Botragy (pronounced boat-RAW-je), on the last day of Passover, police and soldiers went door-to-door and told the Jewish families they had less than 24 hours to pack up and be in front of the town hall early the next morning.

Young Iren was shell-shocked. Three generations of her family had lived in the same house, raising children, cooking meals, putting kids through school, entertaining friends. For decades, this was the only home they had ever known. And now, out of the blue, they were told to leave it all behind except for what each person could fit in a single suitcase.

That night, Leah baked bread and prepared food, all of

which was put in suitcases along with warm clothing, bedding, and other items. The family had a little money and some jewelry to exchange for food if necessary. But then the mayor and the school principal came to the house and demanded that Meyer hand over the money and valuables. Under threat of harm to Meyer and his family, he reluctantly gave it to them.

Iren, now 13, figured escape was impossible for the six Fogel children, who ranged in age from 17 to 7, and their parents. *Our family is too big,* she thought. *Where would we hide? Where would we go? What if my little brothers were separated from the family? Escape is out of the question.*

In the morning, the Fogels silently walked out of the house. As Meyer closed the gate behind him, Iren choked up and wondered, *Will we ever return home again?*

Farmers with horse-drawn wagons brought the Jews of Botragy to the much larger city of Munkacs (pronounced moon-CACH), where thousands of Jews had been rounded up from the area and put in a ghetto. They were all crammed into two brick factories, which were large, drafty warehouses never intended for housing people.

Sanitary conditions were deplorable. The only restroom was an outdoor latrine with no privacy—nothing but a long trench that the men had dug. There was no running water, little food, and no medicine. The sick, the pregnant, and the elderly had to sit on the cold, hard floor. It was so crowded inside that Iren had to walk over other people and their possessions to get to the latrine.

In the middle of the first night, the Germans turned on the lights and shouted, "All men, get up and get out! That includes boys sixteen and over!" Screams of fear and cries of protest echoed throughout the building.

Leah whispered to Moshe, who had just turned 16, and Meyer, "Lie down." Then she grabbed an extra blanket and threw it over them. "You're not going. I'm afraid they'll beat you."

Iren was terrified that if her father and brother were discovered, they—and possibly the whole family—would be killed. For several tense minutes, the soldiers searched the factory and dragged out several men who had tried to hide. Luckily, Meyer and Moshe weren't found. Soon the lights went out and the place quieted down. The next morning, the Fogels learned that the men who were taken outside had been questioned ruthlessly and, in some cases, beaten in a callous effort to collect more money and valuables from them.

Later that day, all girls under the age of 16 were ordered to have their heads shaved, supposedly to prevent lice. Szeren was 17, so she didn't have to follow the edict. Iren stroked her own long blond braids for the last time and submitted to a severe haircut that left her bald. Even though she hadn't consulted her parents, she had followed orders out of fear that if she didn't, the Nazis would harm her or her family. Having faced so many indignities and frightening experiences already, Iren handled this latest humiliation without crying. When her mother saw her bald head, Leah shed a few tears and then handed Iren a scarf to wear. Leah had kept 11-year-old Edit, who had short hair, from getting shaved.

Days later, Meyer's 55-year-old sister Lena, who had lived with the family and was Iren's favorite aunt, passed away in the ghetto from an illness. Iren and her siblings were devastated. "Aunt Lena was a saint," Szeren said. "The only good thing about her death is she doesn't have to suffer and live with fear like we do."

The Fogels spent several weeks in the brick factory before the Nazis began deporting 3,000 Jews a day on a train without their knowing the final destination. When it was the Fogels' turn, they were shoved into a cramped cattle car. During the three-day, two-night trip, Iren wondered, *Where are we going? Why did they take away our identity papers? What will happen to us?*

On the third day, Meyer was looking through a little slit in the boxcar when he announced, "I think we're in Poland."

Iren recalled the rumors about Poland: *The Nazis are mowing down Jews in the fields . . . The Nazis are burning synagogues with Jews trapped inside . . . The Nazis are starving Jews in ghettos.* She heard people whispering in tones that sounded panicky, alarming, and upsetting. A chill coursed through her veins. *What I've heard is probably all true. The Nazis are going to* drop us off in the forest and kill us. How much time do I have left to live?

When the train came to a stop, Iren felt as many passengers did—that death was only minutes away. Meyer peeked through the slit and announced, "It's not a forest! It's a work camp! I see barracks and prisoners in striped uniforms."

People in the boxcar gave shouts and sighs of relief. *They aren't going to kill us*, Iren thought. *They're going to put us to work here, wherever here is.*

It was Auschwitz.

Like all the others brought here, Iren had no idea that Auschwitz was a complex of concentration, extermination, and slave labor camps, including Birkenau and Buna-Monowitz. Nor did they know that most would be dead within the next two hours.

Stepping out of the cattle car to the angry commands of guards, Iren tightened the scarf around her head and held on to the hand of her younger sister, Edit. The guards shouted, "Out! Out, you damn Jews!" "Move! Move!" "Leave your bags behind!"

Immediately, men were separated from the women and children as the guards pushed everyone along on the train platform. It happened so quickly and unexpectedly that there was no time for Iren to say good-bye to her father and Moshe. *Maybe the men will work, and the rest of us will take care of the elderly and the children*, Iren thought.

Iren's mother and two younger brothers, Reuven and Gershon, were shoved to one side with the elderly and children. Iren held Edit's hand even tighter. Seeing Iren in a big coat and a scarf on her head, an SS officer assumed she was older than her true age of 13. In a split second, he pried the two apart and ordered the younger Edit to the left and Iren to the right. Before Iren could take a breath, she lost sight of her little sister, who was caught up in the fast-moving crush of women and children. Iren leaned forward, her eyes searching for Edit, absolutely horrified that her sister was alone in that crowd. Iren's only hope was that Edit would catch up to their mother. *How else will she ever find us in this mob?*

Iren was directed to a group of young women that included Szeren. Utterly petrified at being at the mercy of the horrible guards, Iren felt safer being with her older sister.

After the women were shaved and showered, their left forearms were tattooed with their new identity. Iren was A6236. Without a name or personal documents, she had no proof of her previous existence. She hoped it meant the number was a way to keep track of them.

Iren, Szeren, and 200 other women were moved into a windowless barrack that had no insulation against the heat or cold. Their bed was a wooden slab shared by six inmates. The next day, they were awakened before dawn and made to stand at *Appell* for hours. The SS officers walked up and down the rows, pulling out the very young girls and sick ones they had missed spotting at the train platform. Iren was small for her age, and she feared being selected even though she wasn't sure what it was for. She didn't want to be separated from Szeren. So Iren stood ramrod straight on a rock to make herself appear taller and she pinched her cheeks to get them pink, hoping she would appear healthier. She wasn't chosen, but she remained terrified about future *Selektions*.

Iren asked one of the inmates who had been in Auschwitz for several weeks, "When will we see our family again?"

The prisoner pointed to the chimney of a crematorium and said, "Do you see that smoke? That's where your family is."

"What do you mean?"

"You won't see them again because they were sent to the gas chamber right after they stepped off the train, and then their bodies were cremated."

Iren refused to accept the truth. Walking away, she asked Szeren, "What did the Nazis do to these prisoners to make them say such awful things?"

A month after their arrival, Iren and Szeren were sent to a section of Birkenau where they joined hundreds of female inmates working at a vast warehouse complex next to Crematorium IV. Here, they sifted through huge piles of clothes and possessions of the dead and sorted them for shipment back to Germany for the civilians to use.

To the sisters' good fortune, they reunited with their maternal aunts, Piri and Rozsi Mermelstein, slave laborers in the same warehouse. The aunts, who were in their twenties, became the girls' replacement parents, offering them comfort and encouragement.

Day after day, Iren and Szeren sorted suitcases, eyeglasses, pots and pans, baby carriages, clothing, shoes, food, books, and musical instruments—the last belongings of those sent to the gas chambers. Because the warehouse complex was overflowing with possessions that reached the ceiling and spilled out the doors, the prisoners called it *Kanada* (German for Canada) in the belief that Canada was a wealthy country full of riches.

While separating the belongings, Iren refused to think about the victims because it was too painful. Then one day, she found her aunt Lena's lovely shawl—cashmere and soft—that had always been kept folded in her closet at home, until the deportation. It had been in one of the family's suitcases. Later, Iren came across a pretty white dress with a black flowery design. Her heart sank and her eyes filled with tears because she recognized it immediately. The dress belonged to her mother. Leah had seldom worn it except to the synagogue on high holidays such as Yom Kippur.

As Iren lovingly fingered the fabric, a wave of resignation swept over her that her mother and younger siblings had died in the gas chamber. And yet she still couldn't fully accept it. She refused to put her aunt's shawl or her mother's dress in the pile marked for shipment to Germany. She held them out for a while, but eventually they disappeared.

Like countless times before, Iren looked out the window of the warehouse and saw innocent mothers with their adorable little children sitting passively with their harmless grandparents in the groves at the entrance to the gas chambers. *They think they're going to take showers*, she told herself. *They have no idea what's about to happen to them. They can't imagine the Germans would murder them like this. The Nazis are counting on people believing the Germans are civilized, or they could never get away with it.*

As one of the last people on earth to see the victims of the gas chamber of Crematorium IV alive, Iren had no emotion, no tears, no ache in her gut. Her heart was like a stone. *Why am I not crying? Why aren't my tears flowing? Why can't I feel anymore?*

Losing her feelings was the only way she could cope. She had to pretend the unspeakable atrocities weren't real. *This is not actually on earth*, she would tell herself. *It's a system of masters and slaves, gods and subhumans in some other world.* Iren needed to detach herself from the present just to get through the day because the horror was too overwhelming.

By this time, the gas chambers were operating 24 hours a day. Trains were arriving more frequently, which meant that the mountains of clothes and belongings taken from the victims were growing each day. Even though the workers at *Kanada* were toiling in two 12-hour shifts, they couldn't keep pace. Items were now piling up outside the warehouse, angering the guards, who kept yelling at the prisoners to work faster.

A wire fence separated the *Kanada* workers from the *Sonderkommandos*, Jewish prisoners who, because of their fitness and strength, were forced to handle the corpses. Their job was to haul dead bodies out of the gas chambers and toss them into the crematoriums to burn. Toiling under terrible conditions, the *Sonderkommandos* usually worked for up to four months before they, too, were gassed and tossed into the crematoriums by their replacements, who, in turn, would eventually be killed and replaced in a vicious cycle of death.

Because *Kanada* was near the Auschwitz railroad tracks, Iren was aware of the arrivals of the trains, especially at night when sound carried better than in the day. While sorting clothes, she would hear the whistle and the steam hissing from the locomotive as it pulled in next to the platform. She would listen to the guards barking orders and the new arrivals murmuring in rising intensity. Soon she would see a huge column of unsuspecting women, children, and the elderly moving toward the gas chamber and disappearing on the other side of the gate. And then silence. A few minutes later, she would hear the arrival of another train with the next load of victims.

The *Sonderkommandos* couldn't incinerate the bodies fast enough, so they were ordered to dig pits nearby and burn the corpses outdoors as well. At night, the flames were clearly visible to the doomed new arrivals as they approached the gas chambers. When they saw men tossing bodies into the fire, the people knew they weren't going to the showers to wash; they were going there to die. They screamed and cried and prayed out loud.

Trying to block out their bloodcurdling wails, Iren plugged her ears with her fingers. She just couldn't listen to them moan and weep, knowing those would be the last sounds they would ever make in this life. In a few minutes it would all be silent . . . until the next group.

One day, Iren spotted her aunt Piri, who was always taking chances, inch closer to the fence by Crematorium IV. Iren began trembling, thinking, *If the guard turns around and sees her, he'll shoot her on the spot.* Then Iren saw an 18-year-old boy from Botragy on the other side of the fence edge toward Piri. While the guard still wasn't looking, the boy threw a note over the fence. Piri scooped it up, hid it in her fist, and walked away.

Piri read the note, sighed, and lowered her head. She went up to Iren and Szeren and said, "I just learned that your father had been working as a *Sonderkommando*, but he didn't last long. He was shot and killed. I will spare you the details." There was no word on their brother Moshe's fate.

Once again, Iren dealt with grief in her own way—without feeling. She had to distance herself from the real world. Otherwise, she would stop living or start crying all the time. For many at Birkenau who couldn't deal with their grief, it was so easy, so tempting to take their own life. They simply walked up to the electrified fence when the guard wasn't looking and grabbed on to the wires. Death came quickly, mercifully.

On one level, Iren was fully aware of her family's fate. But on another level, she refused to accept the reality. To help her cope, she often fantasized about returning home and finding her parents and siblings already there, warmly greeting her. She daydreamed of telling the world what was done in Auschwitz-Birkenau, shocking people around the globe until hate, discrimination, and anti-Semitism ended forever.

In January 1945, the SS took thousands of female prisoners—including Iren, Szeren, Piri, and Rozsi—out of Birkenau on a brutal, two-week, 435-mile (700-kilometer) journey to Ravensbrück concentration camp in central Germany. Part of the travel was by open-air cattle car; the rest was by a death march. With no warm clothes and hardly any food or water, they trudged through the bone-numbing cold and snow. Those who fell from exhaustion and couldn't rise were shot dead. During the punishing trek, Piri and Rozsi did all they could to encourage the girls not to give up.

The four survived the death march and arrived in Ravensbrück in early February. Three weeks later, they and other women prisoners were stuffed into open-air cattle cars and shipped toward another camp. Exposed to the relentless winter wind and bitter low temperatures, Iren and the others nearly froze to death.

They were also dehydrated and had no saliva to chew their bread. Thirst was excruciating. During the trip, the train stopped several times to fill up its steam locomotive with water. At one water stop, Piri stood up and dangled her cup over the side, begging someone to fill it. The guard in her cattle car leaped in fury because Piri had the audacity to seek water. He kicked her and beat her until blood streamed down her face. The rest of the prisoners sat quietly. No one said a word, knowing if they protested, they would be beaten, too.

They ended up at another slave labor camp, Neustadt-Glewe (pronounced NOY-shtad GLEE-va), a subcamp of Ravensbrück that held 5,000 women. Physically, mentally, and verbally abused daily, many of the prisoners wasted away because food and water were scarce. Everyone was infested with lice, a condition that triggered a typhus epidemic.

Piri contracted the infectious disease. Suffering from a high fever, she lost her hearing, became delirious, and lurched throughout the barrack, stepping on people and tripping over them. Piri was brought to the infirmary even though many knew the sick there were often taken away and killed. A few days later, Iren and Szeren stood outside the infirmary, peered through the window, and saw Piri indicate she was getting better. But the next time they went to visit her, she was gone.

They were told a truck had taken Piri and other patients away. The girls knew they would never see their aunt again. "If she had been given a few more days, she would have recovered," Iren told Szeren.

For three months at Neustadt-Glewe, the prisoners were barely fed, and suffered from severe malnutrition and dehydration. Rozsi became seriously ill and Szeren was wasting away. At the daily *Appell*, the weakest of the weak were pulled out to await the truck that would take them to another camp for extermination.

By early May, the bareheaded survivors resembled walking skeletons. But some looked worse than others. At an *Appell* in early May, the prisoners stood in line and were closely inspected by the SS officers. Among those selected for the death truck was Szeren.

Iren's mind whirled with shock. She and her sister had been through so much together since their first deportation. *It can't end like this*, Iren thought. *Piri is gone. Rozsi probably won't live much longer. And now they want to take Szeren away to be killed?* Iren's biggest fear—the one terror even greater than death itself—was being left alone. She couldn't bear the thought of being by herself in this heartless, evil world.

I'm not in much better condition than Szeren is. I can't possibly survive without her and Rozsi. Even if I lived long enough to be liberated, how will I get home? Who will help me? What will happen to me?

There was only one option left for Iren. She stepped forward and told the officer, "I am her sister."

The officer looked at Iren's paper-thin frame, nodded, and said, "You can go, too."

Iren gazed at Szeren, who stared back with sad eyes. Not a word was spoken between them. They both understood why it had to be this way.

Iren, Szeren, and other sickly teenagers were put in a locked room to await the truck that would take them to their deaths. Some of the girls wrung their hands and wept. Iren didn't. She had come to terms with her impending death.

By the end of the day, the truck had yet to arrive. Then, suddenly, the door opened. *This is it*, Iren thought. But instead of a guard, a prisoner walked in and said, "No one is around. Get out of here."

Iren, Szeren, and the other girls returned to the barrack where Rozsi, who had been crying and mourning with other prisoners over the supposed death of the girls, sat up and shrieked, "The children are back! The children are back!" It was the first time in a concentration camp that Iren had heard anyone refer to them as children.

The truck never did show up. Over the next few days, the guards acted as if they didn't care about the girls who had been marked for extermination. Then, on May 8, the prisoners woke up and noticed the guard towers were empty. The Nazis had abandoned the camp.

Within hours, Russian soldiers arrived. Rather than bringing the inmates food and medical supplies, the Russians looked around and then left for good. The women and girls would have to fend for themselves, but no one complained for one simple reason:

They were free.

Iren, Szeren, and Rozsi (who was suffering from tuberculosis) found temporary shelter in an empty house in a nearby town. They eventually reached Prague (now the capital of the Czech Republic), where they learned that a few aunts and uncles had survived. Iren and Szeren were the only surviving children, not only from their family but also from their entire hometown of Botragy (now Batrad', Ukraine). No one ever found out what happened to their brother Moshe.

The sisters and Rozsi emigrated to New York in 1947. After marrying a Holocaust survivor whose first wife and two children had been murdered by the Nazis, Rozsi took on the name of Rose Auerhahn and settled in Brooklyn, New York, where she raised two children. Rose, who was in failing health through much of her life, died in 1994. She had six grandchildren.

Szeren, who Americanized her name to Serena, wed Holocaust survivor Eugene Neumann and settled in New Jersey. She has three children and four grandchildren.

Iren, now Irene, married American Martin Weiss in 1949 and they moved to northern Virginia in 1953. She earned a

Bachelor of Arts degree in education from American University and taught in the Fairfax County (VA) Public Schools system for 13 years. Martin passed away in 2013 after 63 years of marriage. Irene has three children, four grandchildren, and one great-grandchild.

Recalls Irene, "When I had my first child, it was such a healing process for me because I was still grieving over the loss of my mother and family. I made a conscious decision to always dress my son beautifully and keep him clean and attractive. I wanted everybody to look at him and smile and give him constant positive feedback, only good vibes, so he would never know what it was like to be treated as a subhuman as I had been."

Several years later, Irene saw a book with a set of photos she never knew existed. They were taken by a Nazi photographer on the day the Fogels arrived at Auschwitz. One of the pictures shows Irene on the Auschwitz railway platform the very moment she was separated from her younger sister, Edit. An even more heartbreaking photo, shot the same day, shows her young brothers Reuven and Gershon in a grove near the crematoriums with their forlorn mother sitting behind them. They were murdered soon after the picture was taken. Irene says that seeing those photos left her "dumbfounded and devastated."

As a volunteer at the United States Holocaust Memorial Museum, Irene speaks to many different groups about her experiences. She also reminds her audiences how effectively the Nazis used propaganda to brainwash people—including millions of children in the Hitler Youth organizations—into believing in anti-Semitism, racism, and militarism. The Nazi message of hate against Jews and others who were deemed enemies of the state was successfully communicated through art, music, theater, films, books, radio, newspapers, and educational materials. "That's how the Nazis were able to motivate so many citizens to accept, turn a blind eye to, or take part in mass exterminations," Irene says. "Today, between social media and the limitless media outlets, people of all ages who lack critical thinking can be easily influenced into believing it's okay to hate or become intolerant of others—and even act on that hatred." She stresses to students the importance of thinking for oneself, checking out the facts, and asking questions. "Hate speech in school, at home, or anywhere is never right."

Irene has made three trips to Auschwitz, some with her children and grandchildren and another as a member of a presidential delegation to mark the seventieth anniversary of the camp's liberation.

In 2015, months before her eighty-fifth birthday, Irene traveled to Lüneburg, Germany, to testify at the trial of former Nazi sergeant Oskar Groening, 94. He was accused of being an accessory to the murders of 300,000 Hungarian Jews in Auschwitz when he was on duty there during a 48-day period in 1944. (The death camp exterminated about 1.2 million people, 90 percent of them Jews.)

The frail, white-haired defendant admitted he was "morally guilty" but insisted that he killed no one at Auschwitz. He claimed he had been on the arrivals ramp "only three or four times" and that his main function was to ship to Nazi headquarters in Berlin the money and possessions of the doomed—a job that earned him the nickname the "Bookkeeper of Auschwitz."

While admitting he had been a compliant and obedient Nazi and SS guard at Auschwitz, Groening denied any personal responsibility for the murder of thousands of men, women, and children. He said he only "contributed to the camp of Auschwitz operating effectively."

Groening told the court he had no right to ask anyone for forgiveness. "I can only ask the Lord God for forgiveness," he said.

In court, Irene said, "The defendant says he does not consider himself a perpetrator but merely a small cog in the machine. But if he were sitting here today in his SS uniform, I would tremble. And all the horror that I experienced as a 13-year-old would return to me. To that 13-year-old, any person who wore that uniform represented terror and the depths to which humanity can sink."

After Irene gave her testimony, she told the press, "He is right that only God can forgive him, because I cannot. He helped murder all the people I loved and cared for. It is never too late to bring people like him to trial."

Groening was found guilty and sentenced to four years in prison.

DELIVERED FROM EVIL

PAULA KOLADICKI

(Paula Burger)

❦

Eight-year-old Paula Koladicki was trembling in terror. She and her three-year-old brother, Isaac, were scrunched inside a closed empty water barrel on the back of a horse-drawn wagon. She was hoping they would sneak past German soldiers who were guarding the ghetto where life had been so cruel to Jews like her.

If something bad happens and we're discovered, we will be killed instantly, she thought. *What if they shoot Isaac first? I'd have to watch him get murdered. No, I can't think such a horrible thought. I must think about escaping.*

Even though Paula was nearly paralyzed with fear, she told herself to stay composed for Isaac's sake. In the dark barrel, she patted his head and rubbed his back to keep him calm and quiet. She could feel the movement of the wagon and hear the clip-clop of the horse's hooves on the cobblestone street.

As the wagon slowed down, Paula sensed they were

nearing the gate manned by armed guards. *If they make the wagon stop and search the barrel, it's all over for us,* she thought. So frightened that she could barely breathe, Paula tried to focus on keeping Isaac silent. That way she wouldn't have to think about the guards. If they knew who was in the barrel, they would have no problem executing the two hidden children. In the Nazi mentality, youth and innocence were not reasons to spare the lives of young Jews. The mounting tension and stuffy air in the barrel nearly made the young girl pass out.

Three years earlier, events had begun unfolding far away that ultimately would change Paula's life and the lives of tens of millions. In August 1939, the cute, pigtailed girl was helping her mother, Sarah, tend to the vegetable garden on the family's sprawling property outside Novogrudek, Poland. At the same time, 510 miles (about 820 kilometers) away in Moscow, Russia, the foreign ministers of Germany and the Soviet Union were meeting in secret, hatching a plot to divide Poland in two. The following month, the Nazis invaded Poland and occupied the western half. Two weeks later, forces of the Soviet Union known as the Red Army took control of the eastern half, which included Novogrudek (now Navahrudak, Belarus). Although the Russians shipped Jews considered political enemies to prisons in Siberia, most of Novogrudek's 6,000 Jews, who made up half the city's population, were treated fairly well.

Paula's father, Wolf, a well-respected businessman, continued to trade in cattle and lumber while running a small grocery store and restaurant with Sarah. Trained as a pharmacist, Sarah was admired for her intelligence and beauty. She gave up her career to work with Wolf and raise their family.

Paula loved exploring the countryside, playing with her cousins and pets, and spending time with her grandmother, Feige Ginienski, who lived with the Koladickis in an impressive home nestled on a large expanse of farmland. The house bustled with a constant flow of visitors—mostly extended family members—as well as a nanny and several peasants who handled many of the day-to-day chores.

With parents who showered her and her baby brother with affection, Paula hardly had a care in the world. By early summer 1941, she couldn't wait to attend first grade in the fall. But in the midst of her childhood fun, Paula detected a change in her parents' mood. A curious child, she was always listening in on grown-ups' conversations. She didn't understand everything they were saying to each other, but she did grasp that they were worried about a Nazi takeover of all of Poland. Whenever she asked serious questions, the adults gently pooh-poohed her, which frustrated her. *Grown-ups talk to me like I'm a toddler*, she would fume to herself. *I'm small, but I'm not stupid.*

In late June 1941, Paula was playing outside her home when German warplanes suddenly appeared in the sky and began bombing Novogrudek, which was slightly more than a mile (about one and a half kilometers) away. As smoke rose over the town and the ground shook, Paula stood transfixed, unaware that several planes were now strafing the family's property. With bullets kicking up dirt close to Paula, her screaming mother yanked her into the house.

Double-crossing the Soviet Union, German forces routed the Red Army in eastern Poland. On July 4, the Nazis marched triumphantly into smoldering Novogrudek and immediately established a series of new anti-Semitic laws.

On July 26, the SS arrived in Novogrudek and demanded that the *Judenrat* (Jewish council) provide the Nazis with enough Jews for a special work detail. After hundreds of people were assembled in the marketplace, the SS picked out 52 Jews—mostly rabbis, doctors, lawyers, and other professionals—and lined them up. While a German band played classical music composed by Johann Strauss, the SS executed all 52 right on the street. Jewish women were then made to wash the blood off the cobblestones.

Every able-bodied Jew from the age of 12 to 60 had to report for work for the Nazi cause. The Germans sent Wolf on mandatory work details building roads. Other Jews were nabbed off the street and told they were being transported to a job, but they never returned. Beatings and killings became commonplace. Children weren't safe, either. Some of Paula's playmates and young cousins soon vanished.

Everyone in the Koladicki family was on edge. Paula was scared all the time without knowing why Jews were being tormented. She didn't have enough knowledge to ask the right questions, not that her parents would answer them anyway, because Wolf and Sarah tried to spare her the awful truth. The fear Paula felt day and night was only marginally eased whenever she snuggled into her parents' comforting arms.

Wolf had a large network of friends and business acquaintances, including Tuvia, Zus, and Asael Bielski, Jewish brothers who were forming a secret resistance movement, which Wolf joined. It meant that he was gone for days at a time. During one of his absences, informants told him of an impending Nazi roundup of Jews in Novogrudek for early December, so Wolf sent word to Sarah to leave the house with their children.

In the middle of the night she woke up Paula and Isaac, made them get dressed, and walked with them in the fierce wind and blowing snow to the home of Polish peasants, where the threesome stayed for several days.

On December 6—while the Koladickis remained in hiding—all Jewish men, women, and children in Novogrudek were required to assemble at the courthouse, where they were forced to stay for two days. Then, on December 8, the Nazis held a *Selektion*—women, children, the sick, and the elderly were put in trucks while people 16 and older who were physically fit or were skilled laborers remained behind. More than

4,000 Jews were transported to a forest outside the nearby village of Skridlevo. In groups of 50, they were ordered to undress in the bitter cold and taken to a ravine where they were shot to death. This tragic day became known as Black Monday.

The remaining 2,000 Jews were taken to the village of Pereshike outside of town and forced to build fences for a ghetto to contain 22 apartment buildings and houses. Each place had to accommodate about 100 persons, making living conditions intolerable.

The Koladickis returned to their home, where they managed to stay during the next four months, hoping they would be ignored. Whenever they were tipped off about an upcoming *Aktion*, they left and hid in peasants' homes—for a price—and then came back when the danger had passed.

Wolf was worried that an anti-Semitic neighbor who wanted the Koladickis' property would one day betray them to the Nazis. That moment came in April 1942 when German officers showed up at their door at night and ordered them to report to the ghetto the following morning, taking only what each member could carry.

Early the next day, the officers arrived to escort the family. Paula's most cherished possession was her doll. It was about nine inches tall and had a ceramic head and arms, and a green dress that Sarah had sewn. The girl put it inside her coat because she didn't want anything bad to happen to it.

Paula kneeled on the floor and kissed her little white

short-haired dog, Lalush, good-bye and wondered what would happen to her beloved pet. She also left behind her box of colored pencils that she had been looking forward to using in school.

As the family walked away from their house under armed guard, Paula searched her parents' faces for reassurance that everything would be all right. They responded with strained smiles and hopeful words they no longer believed. Sarah held Grandmother Feige's hand while Isaac bobbed up and down on Wolf's shoulders. *If we say nothing and do what the Nazis tell us, maybe they'll leave us alone and I can go back to sleeping in my own bed again*, Paula thought.

The Koladickis shared an inhumanely crowded room with strangers in the drab ghetto. Quietly, in an alley behind the apartment where the family lived, Paula and Isaac played hopscotch and hide-and-seek with kids who had escaped the Black Monday massacre. But over time, many playmates disappeared. Paula was aware the Nazis made a sport of hunting down youngsters and dragging them off to be executed. Occasionally, she saw women gather in small circles and weep for the children who had been killed.

There was no doubt in Paula's mind that the Nazis would come for them. Every minute was tinged with that same anxiety, that same relentless worry.

After months in the ghetto, Sarah sat Paula next to her on their small bed and said, "If anything happens to me or your father, promise me you will take care of Isaac." For an eight-year-old, that would be a profound responsibility, one that would weigh heavily on her slender shoulders. But Paula nodded and said, "I promise, Mama. I promise."

As a member of the Bielski partisans, Wolf had been sneaking in and out of the ghetto for months without being detected. When he was tipped off about a new Nazi roundup, he arranged for his children to escape. Late that night, Sarah, who chose to stay behind with her sick mother, handed Paula and Isaac over the ghetto wall to Wolf. The three walked through the night and then, at dawn, set up a camp under a tarp that Wolf tied to a big tree. When they returned to the ghetto a few days later, they learned that hundreds of children had been taken in the roundup.

The next time Wolf was alerted to an impending *Aktion*, he brought Paula and Isaac to a ghetto in the town of Dvorets, 200 miles (322 kilometers) away. They stayed for two weeks until he got word of an upcoming roundup there. "We'll have to sneak out of here and return to the ghetto in Pereshike," he told Paula.

Under a full moon, they escaped Dvorets. As the trio went under a railroad bridge, a squad of Nazis began walking in lockstep across the trestle. Paula was petrified, knowing that if she or Isaac made any kind of sound—a whimper, a cough—they would be discovered. But the two remained as still as statues until the soldiers moved on.

Their return to the Pereshike ghetto was bittersweet. Paula and Isaac were reunited with their mother, but Sarah waited several days before divulging that their grandmother Feige had passed away. Later, Paula overheard women saying that her grandmother was lucky she had died a natural death.

Living in the ghetto was getting harder by the minute. Hunger, illness, lice, murder, beatings, and fear resided there. If there was any hope, it came in the form of news about the Bielski partisans, who had been harassing the Nazis. Hiding out in the forest, Tuvia, Zus, and Asael—whose parents had been murdered on Black Monday—had been slipping into ghettos and recruiting Jews to join their resistance movement. Tuvia held secret meetings in Pereshike, telling people, "We are your only chance."

As a partisan, Wolf left the ghetto for several months and was unable to send any message to his family, which convinced Paula that he was dead.

Her despair soon deepened. On a summer day in 1942, after playing outside in the back alley, Paula went upstairs to her apartment and couldn't find her mother. Her aunt Bella, who lived in the same building, was red-eyed and trembling.

"Where's Mama?" Paula asked.

"Um, she, uh, had to go somewhere," Bella replied, not convincingly.

Having a gut feeling that her mother was in danger, Paula burst into tears. "Where's Mama?" she repeated.

Bella hesitated and then admitted, "The Nazis took her away. They stormed into the building, shouting your father's name. They demanded to know where he was, and your mother said he left months ago. They asked where her children were, and she said she didn't have any. The Nazis pushed her down the stairs and took her away in a truck." Seeing the look of horror on Paula's face, Bella added, "Your mother doesn't know where your father is, so once the Nazis realize that, she will probably be released."

Paula desperately wanted to believe her, desperately wanted the door to open any second and see her mother walk in. But Paula knew better. After all the terrible things the girl had heard about the Nazis, she told herself, *If the Germans arrest you and take you away, you will never be seen again. They don't free you. They kill you.*

Paula didn't have the heart to tell Isaac. She had been his protector, never letting him out of her sight. He could always count on her. And now this eight-year-old girl had to take on the daunting responsibility of looking after her three-year-old brother. For all she knew, they were orphans.

That fall, late one night, a stranger woke Paula from a deep sleep. She was startled but calmed down when he told her that her father was alive. She wanted to shout for joy, but he asked her to remain quiet. "You and your brother must dress quickly," the man whispered. "I am taking you to meet a farmer. Do what he tells you and be silent as the grave. I know that what I am asking of you is frightening, but your father is waiting on the other side."

Paula and Isaac got dressed and followed the stranger out into the street to await the farmer, a gentile whom Wolf trusted. The man had the job of delivering barrels of water into the ghetto in his horse-drawn wagon for the Nazis. On this night, after emptying the barrels, he whispered the two children's names.

Paula grasped Isaac's hand and scurried to the farmer, who was standing by his wagon. He lifted them up one at a time onto the wagon and gently put them inside one of the drained barrels. "You must remain absolutely quiet," he told them. "Don't move. I will get you out of the ghetto." After stuffing a torn blanket around them, he sealed the lid.

Every minute during the journey through the ghetto, Paula worried that they would be discovered. The total darkness inside the barrel and the smell of its moist wood made her think, *This must be what it's like in a coffin.* She hoped it wouldn't be theirs.

The wagon slowed down, which made Paula think they were at the gate. Her heart pounded wildly from the strain of wondering if they would be discovered. She held Isaac tighter, grateful that he was being such a good boy through all of this.

Soon the horse began picking up the pace, and the stress that was squeezing Paula's chest began to ease. From the sound of the hooves, she figured they had cleared the ghetto and were now on a dirt road heading into the country. But she still remained fearful because she was aware German patrols lurked everywhere.

The trip seemed to take forever. Eventually, the wagon stopped. *Is this good or bad?* she wondered. She could hear someone opening the lid. She held her breath, waiting to see who it was. She looked up and, to her great relief, saw the smiling face of the farmer. He hoisted her and Isaac out of the barrel and led them to the hayloft of a barn, where he fed them hard-boiled eggs, dark bread, and water. "Get some sleep," he said softly. "We have a full day of travel tomorrow."

Although Isaac was slumbering, sleep was impossible for Paula. She kept imagining the joy she would soon feel jumping into her father's arms. But that glorious mental picture was repeatedly blotted out by thoughts of the dangers they still faced. *What if someone found out about us? Poles get money for turning Jews over to the Nazis. Any second, Isaac and I could be shot. I wish I were with Papa right now.*

When morning arrived, Paula received a happy surprise. Her 20-year-old cousin Dashke stepped out of the farmhouse. She had escaped from the ghetto the previous night and was going with them to meet up with Wolf and the partisans. Because she was blond and blue-eyed, she could pass for a gentile. Dashke tied a babushka around her head and, pretending to be the farmer's wife, climbed onto the front seat of the wagon.

The farmer made a deep hole in a mound of hay that covered the back of the wagon. "You must hide inside this pile, and then I will cover you up with more hay," he told Paula and Isaac. "No matter what happens, remain quiet and don't move."

The foursome traveled all day without once being stopped by the Nazis. Late that afternoon, the wagon arrived at a remote farmhouse in the forest. The door opened and out flew Wolf, tears running down his face as he picked up both children at the same time, wrapping his strong arms around them. They hugged and kissed and wept.

Wolf then took his children on a horse-drawn wagon deep into the forest. As night fell, Paula started to doze. He nudged her and pointed to a campfire in the distance. "Wake up, Paula," he said. "This is your new home. The Naliboki forest." They had arrived at the main camp of the Bielski Brigade.

The next morning, Paula looked at her new surroundings. Through the filtered sunlight, the forest was bursting with vibrant fall colors of crimson, gold, and emerald. The dew made the grass sparkle like silver filigree. Everywhere she turned, she marveled at subtle hues and shades she had never seen before, and she wished she had her colored pencils and paper to capture nature's beauty.

Most wondrous of all was what Paula no longer saw— German soldiers, guard dogs, and barbed wire fences.

For nearly two years, until summer 1944, when they were liberated, Paula, Isaac, and Wolf remained with the Bielski Brigade, which harassed the enemy by blowing up ammo depots, bridges, and railroad tracks, ambushing convoys and patrols, and helping ghetto survivors escape.

Paula learned that her mother did not die immediately after her arrest in 1942. Because Sarah spoke German and Polish fluently, the Nazis used her as a translator for six weeks. Despite her linguistic skills, however, she was murdered on September 20, which happened to be for Jews the holiest day of the year—Yom Kippur, the Day of Atonement.

After the war, the Koladickis and a widowed member of the Bielski Brigade, named Chana, eventually made their way to the displaced persons camp in Foehrenwald in the American Zone near Munich, Germany. It was 1946. A year later, Wolf and Chana married, and they had a daughter, Fay. In 1949, when Paula was 14, the family obtained visas and emigrated to the United States, settling in Chicago, where Wolf had relatives. Wolf, who ran his own butcher shop for years, died in 1975. Chana died in 1995.

Isaac earned an accounting degree, married, and raised a family. He has served as a professional cantor in synagogues for more than 50 years.

Paula wed in 1951, built a business, and raised three children. Married to her second husband, Sam Burger, Paula lives in Denver, Colorado, and has four children and nine grandchildren. An acclaimed artist, Paula paints bold, colorful landscapes, flowers, abstracts, and Jewish-themed images. Her art has been shown in galleries throughout Colorado, and many of her works are in numerous public, private, and corporate collections.

"I think the reason I survived is so I can tell my story," says Paula, who speaks often at schools and various organizations. "After a talk at one high school, I was approached by a student who said, 'I know what it feels like to lose a mother. My mom was shot and killed by a gang member.' I hugged her and we both cried. I told her that whatever adversity you face, you must find the courage to stand up and keep going and make good of what you have left in your life. That's what I'm hoping to impart to people who learn my story.

"My children and grandchildren see me as a happy, productive, creative person. It's important to have a strong will and a belief to do the best you can with what you have instead of focusing on the negative.

"I have scars on my soul that no bandage can fix, and I have to deal with that. But I stay positive. If I can give hope to a little girl whose mother was killed by a gang, maybe she can look at me and say, 'I can lead a happy, productive life, too.'"

For a personal perspective of Paula's harrowing experiences during the Holocaust, and details about her perilous life as a partisan, read her compelling memoir, Paula's Window: Papa, the Bielski Partisans, and A Life Unexpected (as told to Andrea Jacobs), available on Amazon.com.

THE LIE AND THE BEAR

FREDDIE LESSING

(Dr. Fred Lessing)

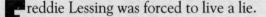

Freddie Lessing was forced to live a lie.

The only way he could survive in the war-torn Netherlands was to pretend he was a sweet, well-behaved Christian boy. Acting sweet and well-behaved was easy because he was already a good kid. But he had to fake being Christian because if people knew the truth—that he was Jewish—he risked extermination.

Given a fictitious background—something about his gentile parents being homeless and needing a place for him to stay while they searched for a permanent home—Freddie was placed with various families throughout the war. From the time he was six years old, he played the part of a good Christian boy flawlessly. If the new family was Protestant, he was Protestant. If they prayed before dinner, he prayed before dinner. If they went to Catholic Mass, he went to Catholic Mass.

In the mind of this little curly-haired lad, the world was black and white—good guys versus bad guys. Freddie knew nothing about history or politics or the reasons for war, just that the Germans and pro-Nazi Dutch were bad, and the British and Americans were good. And the world was dangerous for Jews like him.

More important, he figured out that if he became the quietest, kindest, most courteous little Christian boy in the whole world, he would survive.

Freddie and his brothers Eddie, who was 10 years older, and Attie, who was 2 years older, lived with their parents, Nardus and Engeline "Lien" Lessing, in Delft, Holland. In addition to managing a small clothing store, Nardus was a classical musician who played the piano and cello and gave lessons. Lien, unlike her easygoing husband, was a strong-willed, decisive person who was devoted to the sons she called her golden boys.

In 1940, when Freddie was four years old, the Germans swooped into the Netherlands. They began depriving Jews of their rights and required them to wear stars with *Jood* (Dutch for "Jew") on their clothes. Even though Nardus and Lien were not practicing Jews, they were subject to all anti-Semitic laws. When Nardus was forced to give up his business and house— Jews weren't allowed to own either—the family moved into a three-story leased house that had many rooms, which were rented to local university students. Lien, who was a multi-lingual secretary during the day, cooked dinner for everyone in the house.

Using special lists prepared by Dutch bureaucrats, the Nazis in 1942 began the "resettlement" of Dutch Jews via train to supposed "work camps" in Eastern Europe. These lists included the names and addresses of adult Jews and their children, their places of employment, and even their daily routines, to make it easier for the Nazis to round them up when their time came. Usually, authorities would knock on the door of a Jewish family and give them less than 30 min-utes to leave. To prepare for this train trip at a moment's notice, Lien filled backpacks for each member of the family with necessities such as blankets, clothes, and toiletries. The backpacks were stored in a hallway closet.

Because they were law-abiding citizens who took Germans at their word, most Dutch Jews went on these transports assuming they would work and live in decent conditions. But Nardus and Lien believed otherwise after listening to Freddie's paternal grandfather, Ies, a tailor who lived in Amsterdam. Even though he was Jewish, Ies was exempt from any roundup because he was married to a non-Jew, his second wife. He had heard creditable rumors that Jews weren't being resettled in work camps but were being deported to death camps. He warned Nardus, "Don't go on any transports because you will never come back. The Nazis will kill you."

On the morning of October 23, 1942, Freddie, six, and Attie, eight, were in the attic playing with a windup train when the phone rang. A few minutes later, Lien asked them to come downstairs. They could tell from the anxious, urgent tone in her voice that they weren't being called for breakfast. When the family was together, Lien told the boys, "We have to leave right away because we are all in extreme danger."

Nardus had just received a phone call from Mr. Cohen, an old friend who headed the local Jewish council. Mr. Cohen had told him the Lessings were on the latest roundup list. "The Nazis will be at your door within the next hour or two," Mr. Cohen had warned.

"We're not going," Nardus declared. "To go means certain death."

Lien put her arms around her two youngest sons and said, "You are Jewish boys. And if anyone finds out, they will kill you." No one cried or whined or even asked any questions. The boys understood the situation was serious and scary.

"You must do exactly what we tell you to do," Lien told them. "Trust no one except us and those who we say you can trust." After ripping the stars off their clothes, she said, "You will leave the house now. Just put on your jackets and pretend you're going for a walk. Don't take anything with you."

Freddie was an obedient boy, but this was one time he disobeyed. He grabbed his *beertje*, his little teddy bear that had gone everywhere with him. The six-inch-tall, tan, furry bear looked pitiful because it didn't have a head. Months earlier, the neighbor's dog, a chow chow, had ripped the head off and ate it. Nardus had fastened a small metal disk to the base of the bear's neck so the stuffing, which was made from wood shavings, wouldn't fall out.

Although his *beertje* was headless, it always offered Freddie comfort—and right now, the boy needed it. He knew instinctively that his young childhood was gone forever.

On their parents' instructions, the boys walked to the home of Frits Niewenhuizen and his wife, trusted elderly gentiles. A short while later, Nardus and Lien showed up.

"We are going to hide from the Nazis," Lien told the boys. "Have you ever heard of the term *onderduiken*? It means to dive under, to submerge, and that's what we're going to do from the surface of life. There are five of us, and that's too many to hide in one place. We'll have a much better chance of surviving if we split up and pretend to be someone we're not—non-Jews."

Freddie and Attie were escorted by a young gentile teacher to their grandfather Ies's house in Amsterdam. The boys stayed with him and their step-grandmother, Agaat, and their teenage step-aunt Lia for several months. For Freddie and Attie, this was a fun time because they weren't hidden. Ies took them to the park, the movies, the theater, and the circus. Surprisingly, he had sewn new *Jood* stars on their jackets and sent them out to play, so their Jewish identity was known to the public. What

Ies did was baffling considering Nazis were rounding up Jewish families who lived in the neighborhood.

After Lien obtained false papers, she paid her boys a visit in early 1943 and was horrified and outraged that they were wearing stars. She chewed out Ies, accusing him of jeopardizing their lives: "Why would you put stars on their jackets? I don't care if it is the law or that you are exempt from round-ups. We aren't exempt. The Germans are looking for us, and they know you're Nardus's father and that you live in Amsterdam. It's a miracle they haven't come for the boys."

Lien was so furious she made arrangements for the boys to hide in separate homes—the beginning of a series of sanctuaries for each of them. They were given forged identities that said their last name was Hensink. Told to pose as non-Jews, they became fellow conspirators in a life-or-death charade choreographed by their mother. While their father remained in hiding because he feared he looked "too Jewish," Lien constantly searched for temporary homes for her young boys. Whether it was through telling lies, pulling heartstrings, or relating sob stories, the clever woman was a convincing liar when it came to securing the boys short-term places of safety that lasted sometimes for weeks, sometimes for months.

With forged papers, their older brother, Eddie, worked on farms, pretending to be a non-Jewish teenager. Lien and Nardus moved from place to place, too.

After the younger boys' time with their grandfather, Attie

was placed with a family whose identity was unknown to Freddie. It was better this way. One of the first rules of survival: "The less you know, the better." Rather than eavesdrop on grown-ups' conversations, Freddie tuned them out. That way, if he were ever nabbed and questioned by the Nazis, he could honestly say he didn't know such things as where his parents or siblings were hiding.

Graced with a built-in survival mechanism, Freddie play-acted younger than his age. He carried his little teddy bear with him everywhere, even the dinner table, and often sucked his thumb at the same time. He consciously pretended to be scared and shy—which didn't require much acting at all—so adults wouldn't engage him in conversation, not that they cared what a little boy had to say.

His *beertje* was his only true friend. Freddie lived with strangers who fed him and cared for him. But they were not people he could trust; they were not people who knew he was Jewish. All around him, he felt danger and he needed his silent, fuzzy friend to remain always by his side.

At his first sheltered home, Freddie contracted diphtheria—a serious, and sometimes fatal, bacterial infection that typically causes a sore throat, fever, swollen glands, weakness, and, in severe cases, blockage of the airway. He was so sick that Lien was summoned.

During one of his feverish bouts, he began to hallucinate. He saw scary faces and monsters emerge from the mirrored doors of an armoire and stream toward him. In a panic, Freddie screamed, leaped out of bed, and scampered down the stairs, convinced the monsters were following him. He ran into the living room and right into his mother's arms.

After she calmed him down, she carried him back upstairs and tucked him into bed. "Is there anything you would like?" she asked him.

With a trembling hand, Freddie held up his *beertje* and said, "I want a head for my bear."

Lien took the teddy bear to her hiding place. A few days later, it was returned—with a new head. Lien and Nardus had made the head from the breast pocket of Freddie's gray wool jacket and had stuffed it with pieces of rags. Lien had embroidered the outline of eyes, lips, and nose with red thread and filled in the nose with blue thread. The gray head didn't match the rest of the teddy bear's tan body, but Freddie didn't care. His *beertje* was whole again.

Lien had made arrangements for a doctor to treat Freddie at the house. The boy received six shots, three in each buttock. Because he was circumcised—which all Jewish males were, at a time when most non-Jewish males in Europe weren't—Freddie made sure not to get fully undressed in front of anyone. He knew that if someone noticed, it would lead to the conclusion he was Jewish. Even when he had the shots in his rear end, he disrobed in a way that no one could see he was circumcised.

Shortly after he made a full recovery, Freddie was moved to another family of strangers and then another and another. But he didn't pout. He was still alive, and he felt that, as long as he made people believe he was a Christian, he would stay alive.

By the end of his first year out of reach of the Nazis, Freddie was taken to the city of Tilburg to a boardinghouse full of students, retired people, and women who reminded him of witches.

The owner was a middle-aged woman who was kind to him. A staunch Catholic, she hung a silver crucifix in his room—which was in the attic—and gave him a small bowl that contained holy water. Every day, he dipped his fingers in the water and made the sign of the cross. Because she took him to church, he paid attention to the Catholic rituals. He wasn't bothered by having to follow the traditions of religions other than his own. In fact, doing so bolstered his confidence that he could pass for a Christian.

Despite the number of people in the boardinghouse, Freddie chose to have little contact with them, preferring they would think he was bashful. But this role left him with an empty feeling of loneliness. Alone at night in the attic, Freddie would get in touch with his real self and whisper his deepest thoughts to his *beertje*. This was the only time he allowed himself to think about his family, to be who he really was without pretense. Letting down his guard, he could cry in front of the bear and express his heartache: "When is

Moeder [Dutch for "Mother"] coming back? It's been so long. I miss her."

Holding the teddy bear close to him, he would suck his thumb and rub the bear's paw against his nose. He treasured the bear. It was the one constant in his life, the one tangible connection with his real family, the one stand-in for his mother, father, and brothers.

As she had done for more than a year, Lien risked being caught by the Nazis so she could see Freddie on occasion. During one visit, she saw he was once again deathly ill and having difficulty breathing, so she called a doctor, who examined Freddie at the boardinghouse. The doctor told Lien, "Bundle him up and get him to the hospital immediately. I'll meet you there. He has a serious case of pneumonia."

After six weeks of treatment and recovery, Freddie was released from the hospital. His step-aunt Lia picked him up. When asked where his mother was, she replied, "Your mother broke her leg and is in a hospital in Amsterdam."

Lia took him to a tiny country cottage near the village of Voorthuizen, where, to his boundless delight, he was reunited with his father and two brothers. He learned that during the past year, Attie had been moved from place to place, too. Eddie had eventually joined a group of resistance fighters operating out of a hut in the woods. Nardus had stayed hidden in a place owned by a merchant marine, and, to keep his sanity, had taken up painting.

Freddie was no longer alone; he was with family again. For a year, he had been living with strangers in strange cities and towns, and now here he was at a new place nestled on rolling, gorgeous farmland. The rented two-room cottage had no electricity, no running water, and no bathroom. But it was home—and home meant family.

If only his mother were there. As the weeks went by, he and Attie would ask their father, "When will Moeder be here?" Nardus always conjured up an excuse: Her leg wasn't healing right, so doctors had to break it again, or her leg became infected, requiring lengthy treatment. After a while, the two boys stopped believing him. Although they never said anything to him, they worried that she had been arrested or, even worse, killed. Stuck in Freddie's mind was the thought: *Moeder is gone and we might never see her again.* They kept a picture of Lien on the wall and even though they weren't religious, they always said a daily prayer for her safe return.

During the day, father and sons were busy gathering food and fuel and making enough money to pay for rental of the cottage, which was owned by an anti-Semitic Dutchman who didn't know the family was Jewish. The cottage was situated a few hundred yards from the main house of the landlord and his family.

Nardus sometimes painted pictures of barns and houses for farmers in exchange for money or food. The boys, meanwhile, stole hundreds of the landlord's canning jars—a few at a time—from his shed and sold them to farmers or bartered for food.

At age eight, Freddie learned the rules of living frugally: You never eat the last cookie or the last piece of bread; you always leave something to have later. You don't spend all the money; you save as much as possible. You make things out of objects that other people throw away. And you always look for pieces of wood—no matter how big or small—for the little stove.

After nightfall, Eddie and Nardus would dress in dark clothing, hike to the nearby state forest, and illegally cut down a pine tree with a bow saw. And every day, the younger boys would chop it up. They also had to carry six buckets of water from the well by the main house to the cottage and fill its water tank, which had a faucet. In the fall, the boys would carry empty bags and follow farmers' threshing machines, hoping to collect grain for free. Sometimes they would pay a farmer a few coins to let them fill their bags.

Although they were never starving, the younger boys resorted to begging during the "hunger winter" that blew in at the end of 1944 and lasted until spring 1945. They were in the midst of a severe food shortage throughout the Netherlands.

The boys would go to a farmhouse and exaggerate their situation, playing up how hungry they were. Attie did the talking: "We're from Amsterdam, and you can't believe how bad it is. The streets are filled with bodies. We've fled the city with our parents, but we got separated and we're trying to find them. We're so hungry. Could you please give us something to eat?" Freddie's role was simple: to stand out in the cold and look miserable, which he was, especially since his lips always turned blue.

If the farmer invited them inside to eat, Attie would say, "No, thank you. We need to keep searching for our parents. Can you give us something for us to take?" Usually, the boys would receive a large loaf of bread, cut lengthwise and filled with thick slices of butter or cheese. They would thank the farmer and put the sandwich in a bag and take it home to share with their father and brother.

The boys thought that by faking being hungry and needy, they were pulling the wool over the farmers' eyes. But actually, they weren't fooling other people, because the boys really were hungry and needy. Unable to accept their own reality, they had turned begging into a game so they could cope with their difficult circumstances.

Trying to live as normal a life as possible, Attie and Freddie walked half an hour into the village to attend school. Because classes started with several Christian prayers, the boys deliberately arrived late to avoid reciting them.

German patrols occasionally came through the area, prompting the Lessings to leave the cottage and hide, sometimes overnight, in the woods. It was better to be safe than sorry.

One day, Freddie was playing by the road near the cottage when a farmhand walked by. At the same time, the boy spotted a German soldier riding a bike toward them. Freddie was convinced the soldier would arrest him because Freddie was wearing a pair of overalls that had the words *Lone Ranger* in English—the language of Germany's enemy.

Freddie was too scared to run. Instead, he dropped to the ground so the soldier wouldn't see the writing on the overalls. When Freddie looked up, the soldier was right in front of him on the opposite side of the dirt road. So was the farmhand, who pulled out a gun and ordered the German, "Hands up!" When the soldier reached for his rifle, which was slung over his shoulder, the farmhand shot and killed him. The farmhand kicked the body into a ditch, grabbed the soldier's weapon, hopped on the bike, and rode off.

Shaken by the killing, Freddie dashed to the cottage, which was about 100 feet away. The farmhand, who was actually a resistance fighter, began a gun battle between a hidden squad of his comrades and another German soldier. They killed him, too.

By early 1945, the air war grew more intense over the region. Allied and German aircraft engaged in fierce dogfights that Freddie found scary yet exciting to watch, especially after a plane was shot down and crashed nearby. Once, from about a mile away, he marveled at Allied fighter planes as they dive-bombed and strafed a 100-car-long German ammunition train, destroying it in a series of explosions.

What frightened Freddie the most were the German V-1

flying bombs and the V-2 guided ballistic missiles that soared over the area on their way to Great Britain. The V-1 was known as the buzz bomb because it made a loud buzzing sound. When the engine stopped, the flying bomb would fall and explode. Fortunately, none fell close to the Lessings.

As Allied forces closed in on the Germans in early spring, more bombing from both sides shook the family's cottage. The boys still went to school—until the day they arrived and saw that an errant bomb had destroyed it during the night.

Shortly after one particular bombardment, a farmer showed up and asked Nardus, "Would you people like some chicken? A bomb fell near my chicken coop, and I have all these dead chickens to give away." The Lessings ate well that week.

In April 1945, the countryside became the scene of intense fighting, forcing the Lessings into a bunker by the main house, where they huddled with the landlord and his family. Bombs, grenades, mortar rounds, and gunfire rattled their nerves throughout the day and into the night.

During a lull on the second day of combat, Nardus announced, "We're all hungry. I'm going back to make us some food." He left for the short hike to the cottage. While he was gone, the fighting picked up again. An hour passed, then another. Explosions were getting louder and closer. "He's got to get back here or he'll be killed," Eddie said.

"I'll go get him," Freddie said. "I can run the fastest." He stepped out of the bunker and saw bomb craters and plumes of smoke and fire. Petrified by the continuing blasts and gun-fire, Freddie sprinted to the cottage, threw open the door, and skidded to a stop. There in front of him stood his father, in an apron, calmly cooking on the little stove. "Pappie! You must come to the shelter right now!" Freddie urged.

"I'm almost done frying up chicken and duck," Nardus said. "Be there in a minute."

Freddie had noticed a big change in his father. From a sensitive, philosophical, often impractical man, Nardus had turned into a strong, decisive, courageous man who was focused on keeping his sons alive. He and Freddie—and the food—made it safely to the bunker.

After three days of battle, the gunfire and explosions ceased. From inside the shelter, the inhabitants soon heard unfamiliar mechanical noises like clanking and rumbling. They cautiously stepped outside and saw a wondrous sight—tanks from the Canadian army.

The area was now liberated. No more war. No more hiding. And no more pretending for Freddie. It took a moment before the reality washed over him like a refreshing wave on a hot day at the beach. *It's over!* His head spinning with joy and relief, the nine-year-old boy wished this fantastic feeling could last forever.

He and his brothers sprinted the whole way to Voorthuizen, where deliriously happy villagers were enjoying a spontaneous celebration. Everybody was laughing and hugging. Women in their finest dresses were dancing with loved ones and kissing their liberators. Freddie joined in the fun, but felt a tinge of sadness when he thought about his mother. *I wish she was here to see this.*

The festivities went on for days. Freddie and Attie spent their free time hanging around the Canadian soldiers, who made them their mascots and loaded them up with treats and food.

On May 7, 1945, Allied forces accepted the unconditional surrender of Nazi Germany, officially ending the war in Europe.

The following day, Freddie was playing in the dirt road when he saw his father in the distance. Nardus, who was on a rickety bicycle that had wooden tires, was returning from Voorthuizen with food and a pail of milk dangling from the handlebars. He began yelling and waving and then pedaling faster as milk splashed out of the pail. Freddie couldn't figure out what his father was saying.

But as Nardus drew closer, the boy heard him shout words that filled his heart with pure elation: "Moeder is alive! Moeder is safe!" The glorious news brought Freddie to his knees, and he burst into tears of thankfulness. He couldn't stop crying. None of the boys could after learning their mother had survived the war.

Nardus explained that he had stopped in an office in the village where people were compiling lists of survivors and casualties. Engeline Lessing was on a Red Cross list of refugees at a displaced persons camp in Algiers, Algeria, in northern Africa. Nardus confessed to the younger boys he had known that their mother had been arrested a year earlier. Because he didn't know her fate after the arrest, he had decided to make up stories about her broken leg so the boys wouldn't think she had been murdered.

On May 9, 1944—exactly one year before the family learned she was in Algeria—Lien had left the hospital in Tilburg where Freddie was being treated for pneumonia. When a Dutch policeman, who happened to be a specialist in forgeries, examined her papers, he saw that they were fake and arrested her.

Lien claimed she was an American citizen. (In truth, she wasn't. But she, Nardus, and Eddie had emigrated to the United States in 1929, which was at the beginning of the Great Depression. Unable to survive financially, they had returned to the Netherlands in 1932.) Upon her arrest, she spoke English and told authorities her former address in the United States, the name of the grocery store where she shopped, and the number of the bus she often took. She was so convincing, they believed she was American.

In her possession at the time of her arrest were Freddie's hospital card and papers with the names and addresses of the families who were sheltering her children. When no one was looking, Lien ripped the card and papers into tiny pieces and ate them to keep them out of the hands of the Nazis. Meanwhile, she had managed to bribe a policeman to take a message about her arrest to Lia, who then passed it on to Nardus. In a reply, Nardus hid a message inside a travel-size sewing kit, which Lia was able to get to Lien before she was sent away.

Rather than be executed for being a Jew, Lien was treated as an American prisoner and sent to the Westerbork transit camp in the Netherlands and on to Bergen-Belsen in Germany, where she eventually was included in a prisoner exchange. She was then sent to a United Nations displaced persons camp in Algeria in January 1945, where she spent seven months regaining her health and weight and waiting for the war to end. She sent a telegram to her sister in Holyoke, Massachusetts, asking if there was any news about Nardus and the boys. Meanwhile, Nardus had contacted the same sister asking if she had heard from Lien. The sister managed to put them in touch with each other through letters.

Nardus and the boys moved back to Delft and settled in a house that local authorities had given them and helped furnish with furniture that the Germans had stolen. Late one September night, Eddie was walking along a darkened street by his house when a truck pulled up. A woman leaned out the window and said, "Excuse me, sir, is this Number 32 Maarten Trompstraat?"

Eddie recognized the voice immediately. "Moeder!" he shouted. Lien leaped out of the truck and fell into his arms, weeping and shrieking with joy. Eddie began ringing the doorbell, waking up Nardus, who was annoyed that his sleep was disrupted. When Nardus opened the door, he stared at his wife, burst into sobs of rapture, and hugged her tightly.

Freddie and Attie, who had been sleeping in their room on the third floor, woke up when they heard their mother's voice. Freddie flew down the stairs, while Attie, who was the clumsy brother, stumbled and started to fall, but Lien caught him just in time. They all embraced and kissed and laughed and cried. This was the night of all nights, one showered in euphoria. For the nine-year-old boy who had pined for his mother, it was incredible, miraculous, unbelievable. In fact, he didn't think there was a word that could come close to describing this amazing moment.

After nonstop talking, Lien started to unpack the boxes of goodies she had brought for her boys. As tears trickled down his cheeks, Nardus held up his hand and told her, "Please stop. Just sit there and let me look at you."

The happiness Freddie felt was beyond anything he could have imagined—even greater than the jubilation he felt on the day of liberation, and he hadn't thought anything could top that. But having his mother home sure did. It meant the family was all together again, this time for good.

The Lessing brothers were among the few Jewish children from Delft who survived the Holocaust. Freddie entered fourth grade and returned to a relatively normal childhood. By this time, his beertje *had lost most of its fur, and its stitching was breaking off. But it still was his companion.*

At school and at home, not a word was said about the war. "It was as if it never happened," he recalls today. "There was nothing about the Holocaust, because all the facts hadn't been known yet. But no one talked about it anyway."

In 1948, when Freddie was 12, he (along with his teddy bear), Attie, and Lien emigrated to the United States to join Nardus and Eddie, who had arrived a year earlier. They settled in Springfield, Massachusetts, where Nardus played in the Springfield and Hartford (CT) Symphonies, gave lessons, and performed at weddings and various functions. He died in 1988 at age 88. Lien worked as an executive secretary and volunteered in nursing homes. She died in 1985 at age 85.

Eddie became an industrial designer and a graphic designer. He married a Dutch Holocaust survivor and lived on a kibbutz in Israel for five years before returning to the United States. Living in retirement near New York City, Eddie is an artist whose work often expresses a Holocaust theme. The father of two and grandfather of four, he continues to speak about his experiences to schools and various groups.

After high school in Springfield, Attie (who goes by his Hebrew name, Abba) and Freddie attended different colleges, earned PhDs in philosophy, and became college professors. Abba, who lives in Chicago, retired from Lake Forest College in Illinois and has four children and four grandchildren.

Fred, as he's known now, received his PhD from Yale University and in 1962 became a charter faculty member at Michigan State University-Oakland, which is now Oakland University. He and his second wife, Rosalyn Sherman, a PhD in philosophy, eventually returned to graduate school to become psychologists and then had a therapy practice together in Birmingham, Michigan. Now retired, Fred tells his Holocaust story in visits to schools and organizations. He has four children and seven grandchildren.

"There aren't many child survivors still living," Fred says. "We are the last of the actual witnesses, and we feel a sense of duty to speak."

When Fred attended prep school and college, the teddy bear remained in the care of his mother. Years later, when he was teaching in Michigan, she gave him the beertje, which then sat on a shelf for a long time. In 1991, at a hidden-child conference in New York, Fred brought the teddy bear with him and was struck by the emotional response it created. From then on, whenever he spoke publicly about the Holocaust, he showed off his teddy bear. "I wanted my bear with me to remind me and others that I was just a little kid during the Holocaust," he says.

In 1997, he loaned his beertje to Yad Vashem for a temporary exhibit called No Child's Play, which featured games, toys, and dolls that young survivors had during the Holocaust. The teddy bear was in its own special glass case next to two photos of Freddie when he was five years old. The exhibit was so compelling that it was extended for 18 years.

"I was very hesitant to loan him, but it was the right thing to do," Fred says. "He belongs to history, to Holocaust education. He has always felt like a piece of me, like a child that grows up. In 2007, I went to visit him and had a 'talk' with him. I always refer to him as a person."

The bear has been seen by millions of museum visitors. "Every major leader has been photographed next to the little bear, and it seems to me that it is they who feel the honor," museum director Yehudit Inbar once wrote. "Presidents, prime ministers, tough army generals, all change their expression when they stop at the little glass case."

Says Fred, "I define the Holocaust in terms of the destruction of children and childhood. I speak not only of the million and a half Jewish children who were murdered but also of those who survived. Inside each one, there was a living, breathing, feeling, caring, needing, hoping, loving child who wanted to live freely to grow, to love, to be. The Holocaust represents the fear and hatred of this childlike innocence and freedom of spirit, then and now . . . No belief . . . is more important than the freedom and dignity of a child. If we haven't learned this from the Holocaust, we've learned nothing."

TO BE HUMAN AGAIN

MARTIN WEISS

(Marty Weiss)

────────── ❧ ──────────

For Martin Weiss, the feeling that his life was no longer his own began in 1939 at the age of 10. That's when Hungary invaded and annexed Carpatho-Ukraine (also known as Karpatska Rus), a region of Czechoslovakia where he lived in a loving Orthodox Jewish household.

Because the Hungarian government was aligned with Nazi Germany, the annexed area, including Martin's hometown of Polana (now Polyana, Ukraine), was subject to many of Hitler's anti-Semitic laws that stripped Jews of their businesses and rights as citizens.

The laws changed Martin's young life. The Czech public school was closed, so he had to attend a Russian school because the local population was mostly Russian. Kids he once played with now taunted him, calling him "dirty Jew" as if the phrase were one nasty word. He was furious, but powerless, because all Jews were treated with such contempt.

For the Weiss family to survive financially, he and his brothers had to help their father illegally butcher animals at night and sell the meat on the black market.

Martin lost the companionship of two older brothers, Mendl and Izaak, when they were drafted against their will into Hungarian slave labor battalions. They were shipped to the brutal Russian front, where they were forced to bury the dead and carry out other loathsome tasks.

Over the next few years, the remaining members of his family—his parents, Jacob and Golda, his brother Moshe, his younger sisters, Esther and Miriam, and his older ones, Cilia and Hana—struggled but managed to cope. Like everyone in the family, Martin was grateful for one thing: His other sister, Ellen, had emigrated to the United States just two weeks before the Hungarian takeover. She was now living in the land of the free.

Martin felt the full measure of helplessness in spring 1944. Within weeks of Germany's occupation of Hungary, an estimated 440,000 Jews, including the Weiss family, were rounded up and stuffed in cattle cars, as many as 225 persons per car. They traveled for days without food or water and ended up at a place Martin never heard of—Auschwitz.

Arriving around midnight, they stepped off the train under bright floodlights to face soldiers pointing guns and barking orders—women in this line, men in that line. The angry yells of *Kapos* and the cries from the herded crowd frazzled Martin and left him speechless.

Shuffling in a line, he saw up ahead a steely-eyed SS officer who had been pointing his thumb to the left or right. Judging from the physical stature and age of those sent to the right, Martin, Moshe, and Jacob figured that the group had been chosen for work. *If we're picked, our family will be left alone*, Martin naïvely thought. *They'll be taken care of, and then we'll see them from time to time.*

But he was terrified he wouldn't be selected for work because he saw boys about his size being sent to a different group. At 15, Martin was small for his age. However, he was wearing three coats that added bulk to his slight frame and made him look older. To his relief, he was sent to the labor side with his father and brother. On the women's side, Cilia and Hana were picked for work.

After the *Selektion*, Martin saw his mother and his sisters Esther and Miriam in a group near him. "I'll run over there and join them," he told his father. "They look like they could use some help."

As Martin started running toward them, a *Kapo* in a striped prison uniform grabbed him by the collar and growled, "You can't go there." Raising a broomstick, the *Kapo* threatened, "Get back where you belong or I'll hit you." Then he roughly shoved Martin toward the workers' group.

Returning to his father and brother, Martin complained, "That man was so mean to me."

After being processed and given prison uniforms, those in the new workers group were marched toward the barracks and made to stand outside in the chilly predawn mist. Martin shivered not only from cold but from fear. Gazing at his grim surroundings, he saw flames shooting high above a stand of pine trees in the near distance.

"You see those fires?" a *Kapo* told him. "That's where the rest of your family is."

It was Martin's first indication of the horrible truth that his mother and two little sisters had been gassed and cremated.

After 10 awful days at the death camp, Martin was put in a cattle car with 49 other Jewish prisoners, including his father, uncles Zalman and Elje (Jacob's brothers), and teenage cousins Erno and Mayer. His brother Moshe was separated from them. For three days, they sat cross-legged in a slow train chugging somewhere westbound. They weren't allowed to move or talk. Given no food or water, all they had were hunger pangs, parched throats, and their own thoughts. *If I had to paint a picture of hell, I would paint Auschwitz*, Martin told himself.

Eventually, the train reached its final destination—Mauthausen (pronounced MOT-how-zin). It was one of the Nazis' largest concentration camp complexes, holding tens of thousands of Jews, Russian POWs, German criminals, political prisoners, Gypsies, and Jehovah's Witnesses (people of faith who refused to give their loyalty to Hitler). The Nazis nicknamed the camp *Knockenmuhle* (German for "bone-grinder") because of its reputation for working its slave laborers to death. The subcamps of the complex included arms and munitions factories.

From the train, Martin and his fellow prisoners were marched up a hill and through a gate of Mauthausen's imposing stone-walled fortress, where the humiliation began. Upon arrival, they were stripped of their names. He was no longer Martin Weiss. He was 68912—a number stamped on a small piece of sheet metal that was wrapped around his wrist with wire to form a bracelet.

Mistreatment was an everyday occurrence: The new arrivals were forced to stand at *Appell* for hours on end in the broiling sun. In the evening, prisoners had to run inside their barrack the moment the *Kapos* blew their whistles and opened the door. Standing on each side of the doorway, the *Kapos* used broomsticks to smack the slowest inmates. Once the prisoners were inside, half stood against one wall while the other half stood by the opposite wall. Mattresses covered the floor, with no space between them. When the *Kapos* blew their whistles again, the prisoners flopped onto the mattresses so that when they went to sleep, one person's feet were in the face of the other person. In the morning, when the *Kapos* blew their whistles, the inmates who were the last to get up, get out, and stand at *Appell* were walloped hard with the broomsticks.

Martin contracted a serious eye infection that would go untreated for more than a year. Every morning he would need to clean out the pus that had glued his diseased eye shut during the night.

After spending a couple of weeks in Mauthausen, Martin, his father, Jacob, his uncle Elje, and his cousins Erno and Mayer were shipped off to a subcamp in the city of Melk about 50 miles (80 kilometers) away. It was a smaller version of the main camp but with just as much misery and degradation. Like Mauthausen, Melk was populated with thousands of political prisoners besides Hungarian Jews, including Polish Jews, Catholic Poles, Serbians, Ukrainians, Greeks, Italians, and some Spaniards. Electrified and barbed wire fences wrapped around a perimeter dotted with watchtowers.

Inmates were taken by a work train to an imposing mountain, where they burrowed tunnels and carved caverns that the Nazis planned to turn into underground arms factories. The men toiled under the supervision of civilian workers and *Kapos*, many of them cruel goons who excelled at abuse. Whippings and beatings were plentiful; not so for food and water.

Because Martin was put on a different work shift from his other family members, he seldom saw his father. During their infrequent meetings, Martin noticed Jacob's physical condition worsen, so the boy offered to share his bread with him. Jacob not only refused but tried to give a portion of his bread to Martin. They were always trying to help each other, and the same was true of his uncle and cousins. That wasn't always the case among other inmates. Martin once saw a father and son get into a fight over a piece of bread.

On a typical day, Martin and the other prisoners stood on the parade ground, where they were counted five or six times. Then they were led out of the camp gate and counted again at the boarding platform of the work train. Once at the tunnels, they were counted a third time. After work, they were counted as they exited the tunnels, then at the boarding platform, and again back in the camp. "The way they constantly count us, you'd think we were their most prized possessions," Martin told Erno.

Digging tunnels was dangerous work. Because the mountain consisted of fine sand and quartz, the earth was soft, so cave-ins were frequent. It wasn't unusual for dozens of prisoners at a time to end up buried alive. Sometimes they were saved; many times they weren't.

Even though Martin was slender and underage, he shoveled sand and stones onto a conveyor belt just as bigger and older inmates did. Occasionally, he mixed cement and poured it into pails for workers on scaffolding to pull up on ropes.

Slaving away on these 12-hour shifts taxed his frail body, but he persevered. *You just have to accept it,* he told himself. *You just have to make it through the day.*

On July 8, 1944, Martin was selected with several other inmates for a special detail. They were marched about two miles (three kilometers) to a field where they were ordered to clear it of brush, fallen twigs, and branches. Having labored in the tunnels, Martin was only too happy to work outside because the sun was shining, the air was fresh, and the breeze was cool. *This is the best job I could hope for,* he thought. *It's a beautiful day, and I'm not surrounded by barbed wire or an electrified fence. It's like I'm not a prisoner.*

About noon, he began hearing a droning noise above that kept intensifying. Martin looked up and saw they were Allied bombers. As the planes thundered by, he cheered silently, knowing that if he showed any expression or gesture of support for the Allies, he would be severely punished. Martin didn't care if the planes dropped their bombs right there, figuring the Nazis would eventually kill him anyway.

But the planes flew on. Seconds later, however, he heard bombs exploding in the direction of the camp. When he returned to Melk, he saw that his barrack—a large reinforced concrete building that at one time had been an ammunition depot—was bombed. As one of the camp's biggest buildings, it accommodated about 1,000 prisoners, but now half of it was destroyed and more than 500 prisoners inside had been killed. (The pilots had been told, erroneously, that the concrete barrack was still an ammunition depot.)

If I hadn't been chosen to work in the fields today, I probably would've been one of the victims, Martin thought.

Erno was in the barrack when it was bombed, but in the far end that wasn't damaged. However, he was still slightly wounded. It happened when he heard the planes, looked out the window, saw they were the Allies, and cheered. Seeing Erno rooting for the Allies, a guard shot at him. One of the bullets chipped a piece of concrete, which tore into Erno's arm. So, too, did a fragment from a ricocheting bullet.

Jacob, Elje, and Mayer were not injured in the bombing because they were in a wooden barrack on the other side of the camp.

Weeks later, Martin was working the night shift when he walked out of the tunnel about 7:30 a.m. to use the latrine, which was a few hundred yards away. Ten minutes later, as he was returning, he saw heavy black smoke pouring out of the tunnel entrance. An electrical cable had caught fire inside. The smoke was so thick it blotted out the tunnel's bare lightbulbs, making it impossible for many of the workers to find their way to safety. Some of those on scaffolding inside blindly jumped down onto a moving conveyor belt to get out. But 75 prisoners died, most from smoke inhalation. *That's my second close call with death here*, Martin thought. *I picked the right time to go to the latrine.*

Martin realized just how fickle life could be—and how lucky he was to be alive. What if he hadn't been chosen to work in the fields on the day his barrack was bombed? What if he hadn't gone to relieve himself when the deadly fire broke out in the tunnel? And didn't he twice cheat death upon his arrival in Auschwitz? The first time by wearing three coats to make him look older. And the second time when the *Kapo* shoved him back toward the workers' group.

Whatever luck he thought blessed him had diminished by late summer, because all the slave laborers like Martin were suffering from dehydration and malnutrition. He was always hungry. Eating real food was what he and his comrades talked about more than anything else.

At noon, the inmates received the main meal of the day—a disgusting brew that passed for spinach soup or vegetable stew and was brought out in garbage cans. With each sip of spinach soup, Martin would get a mouthful of sand. The soup gave many inmates dysentery, often leading to the death of the weaker ones.

Other times, prisoners were given a stew made of carrots with tops almost too bitter for Martin to swallow. On hot days, when the cover was lifted off the top of the garbage can, the stew would bubble from fermentation. The smell was enough to make Martin vomit, but he ate it anyway. Hunger will do that to a starving person.

Erno never went hungry after becoming the orderly for a

Kapo, a fierce-looking, tattooed German who had been convicted of murder. As an orderly, Erno received extra food. He also wore a tailor-made prison uniform and had access to soap and showers.

Taking advantage of his position, Erno got Martin a short-term job peeling potatoes—work Martin loved because it kept him out of the tunnels. His kitchen duty required him to carve thick peels, leaving only the heart of the potatoes, which were for the consumption of the SS officers only. The heartless Nazis would not let the famished kitchen help eat the peelings or use them in a stew for the prisoners. The peelings had to be thrown out.

Hunger spurred Martin to take a perilous risk. He would secretly cut slices of potatoes and slip them inside his pants at the waist. Using a string for a belt, he would tightly cinch his pants, holding the slices in place against his skin until he met up with his relatives and shared the potato pieces with them. *If the guards catch me, it'll be over for me*, Martin thought. *But I have to do it. Anything to help us stay alive.*

Occasionally, throughout the summer, prisoners washed their lice-infested clothes with only water because they weren't given soap. When the inmates dried the clothes outside, they discovered the lice thrived in the sunshine and had multiplied. "Why bother washing?" Martin told his comrades. "It doesn't do any good. The lice are literally eating us alive."

Work and sleep. Hunger and exhaustion. That was Martin's life. That was everyone's life at Melk. Sometimes a worker was so dog-tired he fell asleep in the tunnel. When that happened and he failed to show up for *Appell* at the end of his shift, the rest of the bushed slave laborers were forced to stand outside in the rain, cold, heat, or wind for hours while guards searched for the missing prisoner. If the guards found him and woke him up, they would beat him mercilessly, sometimes to death. If he had died from fatigue or illness in the tunnel, they wouldn't care. But under no circumstances would the guards take the rest of the exhausted prisoners back to the camp until all were accounted for, dead or alive.

Martin never got enough rest. Sometimes when he felt too drained and weary to move at the end of his shift, he dozed off while still on his feet on his way to the work train. Once a week, he and his 500 barrack mates had to stand in line to get a haircut after putting in a full 12 hours of work. Instead of electric clippers, the barber used much slower hand clippers. He would shave a strip from the forehead to the back of the scalp so the prisoner would be easily recognized by the public if he escaped. During these long, tedious waits for haircuts, Martin snoozed while shuffling his feet.

When winter set in and the winds howled and the temperatures plunged below zero, prisoners had nothing other than their thin shirts to keep them warm. For insulation, some inmates cut holes in empty cement bags and wore them under their shirts even though the bags still had traces of powdered cement in them that irritated the skin and caused rashes. Wearing the bags was against camp rules.

Often when Martin and his fellow tired slave laborers arrived at camp around 1:00 a.m. after another backbreaking work shift, the commandant would show up and make them stand at attention in the freezing cold. He would order guards to check the prisoners for cement bags under their clothes. Any inmate who wore a bag received 25 lashes with a bull-whip. When the flogging was finished, the prisoner wished he were dead. Sometimes he was.

Wanting nothing more than to sleep, the workers had to listen to the late-night rants of the commandant, who tried to talk like Hitler. He bullied and threatened prisoners. To Martin, the man sounded less like the *Führer* and more like a mad dog.

The camp had an infirmary staffed by a doctor who was also a prisoner. It had few medical supplies to help the sick and injured. Any inmate who went to the infirmary seldom returned to his barrack. If a slave laborer couldn't work, he was of no use to the Nazis.

Martin's cousin Mayer, who was 16, was rolling a big fly-wheel—a heavy steel disk that helps power a machine—up a slight incline when he slipped. The flywheel rolled back, knocked him down, and crushed his ankle. He was taken to the infirmary and was never seen again. A prisoner told

Martin, "If you don't die in the infirmary, you die in the gas chamber."

In January 1945, Martin went to the other side of the camp, hoping to see his father. Instead, he found his uncle Elje, teary-eyed and trembling. Elje delivered tragic news: Jacob had died three days earlier from pneumonia aggravated by hunger and exhaustion. Even though Martin was close to his father, the boy was too sapped of any emotion to cry. He couldn't shed a single tear because the concentration camps had stripped him of any feelings of a normal human being. There was nothing left inside him. Elje, who didn't have any children, was Martin's godfather and favored him over the other nephews. The sorrow he felt for Martin was compounded by his own grief over the death of his brother and best friend.

To the Nazis at Melk, Jacob was merely another body to dispose of. By now, 3,000 new prisoners were being brought into the camp every month to replace the ones who had died.

Martin stayed out of trouble with the guards because he followed the rules. And he certainly didn't want to face any punishment doled out by the homicidal *Kapo* Erno worked for. Martin steered clear of him.

During *Appell*, Martin tried to avoid being in the front or back of any line because his goal was to go unnoticed by the guards and *Kapos*. But one blustery winter day, he wound up at the end of a row on the platform for the work train. A new captain of the guard was walking by and eyed Martin. The officer had something in his hand and started to extend his arm. Martin braced himself, expecting to receive a painful body blow. Without saying a word or slowing his pace, the officer handed him a piece of bread and kept on walking. It was the only act of kindness from an officer that Martin ever experienced at this or any camp.

As the Red Army advanced toward Melk in early April 1945, many of the prisoners, including Martin, were shipped back to Mauthausen. *Now it's our turn to die*, Martin thought. *They're going to execute us.*

The Nazis instead sent the Jewish prisoners out of Mauthausen again. Most, including Elje and Erno, went to the Ebensee subcamp. Split from his remaining family members and feeling terribly lonely, Martin was sent on a death march with another group of fellow Jews.

For food, they were given a piece of black bread that included sawdust filler, and tea made from sugar beets meant for cattle feed. Because the bread would crumble when cut, servers had to ladle it onto the palms of the prisoners. Martin ate the bread even though it was often speckled with green, white, and blue mold.

Given hardly any food or water, many were too weak to walk and were shot. After trekking for several harsh days, Martin was growing weaker and had to focus solely on putting one foot in front of the other to avoid dying from a bullet to the head. His malnourished body craved fuel—grass, roots, leaves, anything.

When two prisoners next to Martin spotted a potato lying on the road, they reached for it at the same time. Too crazed and starved to share the potato, they began fighting over it. A Wehrmacht guard put an end to the scuffle. He shot one of them. For all the cruelty Martin had witnessed in his young life, he was still shocked by the brazen murder.

After marching more than 30 miles (48 kilometers), the men arrived at Gunskirchen Lager (pronounced GURNZ-keer-chin LAW-ger), a subcamp of Mauthausen, where the conditions stretched the definition of the word sickening. About 15,000 prisoners were squeezed into five one-story frame barracks designed for only 1,000 inmates each. There were no bunks, so 3,000 inmates in each barrack had to sleep standing up. Because of his small build, Martin was able to doze in a crouched position. It wasn't uncommon for an inmate to wake up in the morning and find a dead person pressed against him.

Despite seemingly impossible odds, Martin bumped into his 22-year-old cousin Jeno Weiss, who was Erno's brother. He had just arrived from a Hungarian labor battalion. No longer feeling lonely, Martin was ecstatic to once again have a family member by his side. Jeno, who was in decent physical condition compared to most inmates, offered Martin comfort and support.

Martin had wasted away to 75 pounds but was still in better shape than many of the scrawny prisoners who were lurching around like zombies. Almost daily, he encountered a common sight: A frail inmate shuffled along and plopped facefirst into a mud puddle. Too weak to even move his head, he had just enough strength to lift his shaky hand a few inches in a signal for help. But no one came to his aid. They let him die. To Martin, it was more compassionate this way. *He's so far gone he's better off dying sooner rather than later. He's done suffering.*

Martin would help those he thought had a chance to live—the ones who hobbled along, leaning on sticks, crude crutches, or each other. Lice, insects, and even vermin crawled over them.

The stench hung over the camp like a nauseating fog—a disgusting mixture of smells from excrement, urine, body odors, trash fires, and even decomposing corpses.

Martin felt like so many captives did: They were subhuman. The inmates were so far removed from a civilized world—from anything even remotely civilized—that there was no other way for them to think of themselves. *I feel like an animal*, Martin thought. *No, even less than that.* He was just biding his time until he withered away.

On May 4, 1945, the prisoners woke up and discovered the guards were gone. But Martin and many others were afraid to leave the camp because they thought it was a trap.

"The Germans probably have machine guns out there just waiting to mow us down when we step outside," Martin said. The inmates spent the rest of the day and night in the camp.

Spurred by hunger, Martin, Jeno, and three others ventured out together in search of food the next day. Keeping a wary eye out for the guards, they walked into the countryside—and, to their great elation, saw American soldiers. It was then that Martin realized he was no longer under German oppression. "I can't believe the Nazis didn't kill us," Martin said. "I never thought that we'd be free."

Martin's joy on his first day of freedom was tainted by his hatred of all Germans. "Every German is a Nazi, and every Nazi deserves to die," he told his comrades, who nodded in agreement. "They treated us like animals, so we might as well act like animals. If I had a gun right now, I'd shoot every German I saw."

They eventually found an abandoned army truck. Looking through the window, they saw a bowl of lard on the front seat. "We can use this to cook with," Jeno said.

"Cook what?" Martin asked.

"We'll go to a farm and get the ingredients to make dumplings," Jeno replied.

One of the men smashed the truck's window with his fist and opened the door. They whooped with delight when they found a stack of refined animal hides in the back. "We can take some of these to a shoemaker and have him make us real shoes," said Jeno.

"And we can use the hides to trade for food," Martin added.

After each person took as many hides as he could carry, they continued their quest for food and soon spotted a farmhouse. As they approached it, Martin could feel the anger welling up inside him. Even though he had little strength, he knew it would be easy for them to barge into the house and steal all the food. *The Germans did it to the Jews all the time,* he rationalized.

For Martin and his comrades, the primal urge to vent their rage on whoever was inside the house seemed tempting. How satisfying it would feel to unleash their wrath like the abused wild animals the Nazis had turned them into. So what if they were physically weak? Their fury would power them.

They knocked on the door. A woman opened it just a crack and timidly asked what they wanted. To their surprise, something deep within their souls clamped a lid on their boiling anger, resentment, and outrage. No one in the group shoved the woman down and burst into the house. No one threatened her or made demands. They simply asked her for some eggs, flour, and water. She gave them the food, and they went to the barn, where a kettle dangled over a pile of firewood. They started a fire and, by mixing the ingredients with lard in the kettle, made dumplings.

Nothing had tasted so good to Martin since he had devoured his mother's last home-cooked meal—the one before the deportations, before the end of the life he once knew. As much as he wanted to devour a few dozen dumplings, Martin was smart enough to limit his food intake so his stomach could get used to real food. The oldest in the group, Hershel, the 55-year-old uncle of one of the men, couldn't resist and wolfed down all he could.

When they finished eating, one of them said, "You know what we should do? Take some hides and give them to the lady."

The suggestion tapped into each of their individual reservoirs of morality. The code of ethics they had been raised with—the one that had been buried during their captivity—was now bubbling to the surface. Without much conversation, they walked up to the door, gave hides to the lady as payment for the food, and thanked her.

And with that simple act of appreciation and thoughtfulness, Martin felt something he hadn't felt in a long, long time. He felt like a human being again.

On May 4, 1945, American forces liberated Gunskirchen Lager after an officer of the camp surrendered. He showed them orders he had been given earlier from the German high command to kill all the prisoners, but he had refused to carry out the mass executions.

After spending the first night of freedom in the German woman's barn, Martin and his four comrades walked to a US Army camp, where they were fed, deloused, and given fresh clothes. Sadly, Hershel died because his stomach couldn't handle the food he had consumed.

Martin became ill with an extremely high fever that left him unable to swallow. After a three-week recovery, he and Jeno decided to return to Polana even though they had no money. They walked partway and sneaked onto trains—sometimes while sitting on the roofs of passenger cars. Along the way, Martin bumped into an acquaintance who told him his brother Mendl had escaped from a Hungarian labor battalion and was living in a town now known as Bilky, Ukraine. While Martin went to look for Mendl, Jeno met up with his uncles Elje and Zalman and brother Erno in Polana. They eventually emigrated to the United States.

Meanwhile, Martin found Mendl. A few months later, in Prague (now the capital of the Czech Republic), they reunited with their sister Cilia. She had been liberated in April 1945 by the British at the concentration camp in Bergen-Belsen, Germany, where she and their sister Hana had been taken shortly after arriving in Auschwitz. She said Hana had died at Bergen-Belsen from typhus.

They also learned that their brother Moshe had survived the concentration camps. But shortly after liberation, Moshe confronted a man from their hometown and threatened to expose him for being a vicious Kapo. Moshe disappeared the next day. He was last seen with the former Kapo, who denied any knowledge of Moshe's fate.

While their brother Izaak was in a Hungarian labor battalion, he was wrongly accused by the Russians of being a German spy and was held captive in a Russian POW camp until his release in 1947—two years after the war was over. He eventually married and raised a family in California.

Their sister Ellen, who had been living in the United States since 1939, arranged for visas for Martin, Mendl, Cilia, and Cilia's husband, Nandor. They arrived in New York City in 1946.

Within three weeks, Martin settled in Carteret, New Jersey, where Ellen and her husband, Willie, lived. Martin, who didn't speak a word of English, began attending night school to learn the language. He landed a job and moved into his own place. "I just wanted to blend into society and be a normal citizen," he recalls. "I didn't want any special attention or anyone to feel sorry for me because I didn't want to go through life as a victim." He chose not to talk about his Holocaust experience with his siblings.

Martin was drafted into the US Army and served during the Korean War. During his military stint, he was granted American citizenship. After his discharge from the army, he began a long career in the grocery business. In 1957, he married and, with his wife, Joan, raised two children. After Martin retired, he and Joan moved to Bethesda, Maryland, so they could watch some of their four grandchildren grow up.

In 1998, Marty, as his friends and family call him, began volunteering at the United States Holocaust Memorial Museum. He is not related to Holocaust survivor and museum volunteer Irene Weiss, whose story is featured earlier in this book. Her late husband was also named Martin Weiss.

"I didn't talk to my wife or kids about the Holocaust for years," Marty says. "In fact, the first time I spoke publicly about it was when I volunteered at the Holocaust museum. My daughter was 46 years old, hearing me talk about it for the first time."

One of the points Martin makes when he talks to groups is that hate festers in people who dehumanize others. "When the Nazis and their sympathizers thought of the Jews and other prisoners as less than human, it was much easier to kill them," he says. "It's not so easy to do when they are viewed as equals, as humans."

THE EDGE OF DESPERATION

RÓZIA GROSMAN

(Rose Gelbart)

———————— ❧ ————————

Standing precariously on the edge of an apartment building rooftop, nine-year-old Rózia Grosman felt her mother's trembling hand squeeze hers tightly. The little girl had never before seen that look in her mother's eyes. It was beyond sadness, beyond anguish.

From her vantage point five stories up, Rózia saw police cars—their sirens blaring—a block away and speeding toward them. *Is this why we're up here?* she wondered. *Are they coming for us?*

Ever since the Nazis invaded Poland, Rózia's childhood had been nothing more than weeks and months and years of hide-and-seek—only this wasn't a game. It was a daily life-and-death challenge for the little Jewish girl who, like millions of others, was trapped in a world gone mad. Sneak here, run there. Stay in this apartment, hole up in that farmhouse. Go with this stranger, live with that stranger. Don't open the door. Don't peek out the window. And don't call your mother Mother.

It was all so confusing, so frightening. Rózia didn't fully understand the reasons why she had to run from the Germans or why she had to hide from them. She just knew the Nazis wanted her and her mother dead.

As the police cars slowed down near the building, Rózia could feel the fear slithering throughout her body. She was too scared to ask, "Mama? What are we doing here?"

Had her mother revealed the truth, Rózia would have been even more terrified of the answer: "If they come for us, we will jump to our deaths together."

In the Polish city of Kalisz (pronounced KAH-leesh), Rózia lived with her parents in a fashionable apartment decorated with custom-made furniture. Sleeping in sheets of blue satin trimmed in lace in a bedroom with white lacquered furniture, Rózia felt like a princess. She was doted on not only by her parents but also by her nanny and housekeeper and her extended family of grandparents, aunts, uncles, and cousins.

Her father, Jozef, ran a profitable company that made shoes for women and children in a busy workshop with 10 employees. Her mother, Sabina, was a sharp businesswoman who visited area shops, selling the shoes as well as fabric from her own thriving textile business.

On Rózia's fourth birthday in January 1939, her parents

threw a big party for her. All the family members attended, including her cousin and best friend, Belusia, who was a few months younger. The two girls looked so much alike they could pass for twins, especially when they were dressed in identical outfits. The only difference between them was that Rózia had blue eyes and blond hair, and Belusia had brown eyes and black hair.

But Rózia's idyllic life was shattered when the Germans invaded Poland in September that year. Thousands fled the city, including the Grosmans. As the family headed east on foot with hordes of refugees crowding the roads, roaring German planes dived on them, unleashing thousands of machine gun rounds. In the eyes of a four-year-old girl, the planes looked like gigantic, fierce birds. Rózia watched in horror as people and animals were struck down. Death was everywhere she looked.

Suddenly, a plane came in low over the road and began firing its machine guns. Her uncle, Szymek Langner, grabbed her hand, threw her in a ditch, and shielded her with his body. Bullets plowed into the ground near them, but the two weren't hurt. After the plane zoomed off, Rózia heard only silence for a few seconds before the moans of the wounded and wails for the dead filled the air.

This was the little girl's first taste of war, and it was bitter. After Poland surrendered weeks later, the Grosmans returned to their apartment. It was only a short time until the Nazis showed up at night and demanded the family evacuate immediately. "You have twenty minutes to pack up and find another place to live," an SS officer told them. "We are taking over this apartment."

Jozef woke up Rózia. Still in her pajamas, the frightened girl locked her arms around his neck as he carried her across town to her grandparents' apartment. Other relatives had gathered there, fearing more trouble awaited the Jews of Kalisz. Seeing her cousin Belusia, Rózia forgot all about being afraid, and the girls began jumping up and down on the bed. But their fun was cut short when four German soldiers burst into the apartment and brandished their rifles. Everyone froze.

"Show up at the marketplace," one of the soldiers snapped. "You won't be coming back here, so take only what you can carry. You have twenty minutes."

Rózia was so scared her mind went blank. Soon, the Grosmans and other family members arrived at the marketplace, where they were kept all night while the Nazis rummaged through the Jews' bags, stealing anything of value. Then families were split up. Most of Rózia's relatives, including Belusia, were sent to the Polish city of Rzeszow (pronounced JESHZ-ov). The Grosmans were shipped to Warsaw.

In January 1940, after Sabina obtained permission from the Nazis, the Grosmans joined their relatives in the Jewish neighborhood in Rzeszow, moving into a terribly overcrowded house with dozens of strangers.

While her parents had to register for work, Rózia, who had just turned five, sat on the curb with Belusia. Asked if she felt like playing, Rózia shook her head and said, "I think something bad is happening." Then, trying to perk up, she added with a smile, "But I'm happy to be here with you again, Belusia."

By now, the Nazis had destroyed most of the synagogues in the city. Jews were forced to pull down the walls of an old Jewish cemetery, break up all the tombstones, and pave roads with the rubble. The former cemetery was turned into the *Sammelplatz*, a place where people assembled. Nazis made Orthodox Jews clean the streets on their hands and knees, and soldiers also cut or pulled off the men's beards and earlocks (side curls).

Slave laborers had to work for the Nazis. Jozef was assigned to make boots for high-ranking Gestapo officers, while Sabina was put on a road crew that laid culverts. In the evening, she cleaned the SS officers' club and usually returned home around midnight. The only advantage to the night job was the opportunity to bring home food items like eggs or butter, keeping some and selling the rest on the black market. Because she worked outside the ghetto, Sabina often sold other Jews' valuables and used the money to buy food for the people.

Uncle Szymek, who was married and had an infant son, worked as a locksmith. One of his tasks was making locks for crates to hold gold, silver, and diamonds that the Nazis had stolen from Jews and were shipping back to private homes in Germany. Sabina's sisters, Rozia, who was Belusia's mother, and Balbina, were seamstresses. Belusia's father had fled to the Soviet Union and was never heard from again.

In January 1942, days after Rózia's seventh birthday, the Nazis enclosed the Jewish neighborhood with barbed wire and divided it into two ghettos. Generally, those like Jozef and Sabina, who had jobs considered essential to the Nazis, lived with their children in the smaller ghetto, while the rest, including single mothers with children, like Rózia's aunts, lived in the larger ghetto. The divided ghettos meant that Rózia couldn't see Belusia anymore.

More than 12,000 Jews in the two ghettos were now at the mercy of the Germans, who began limiting the supply of food, medicine, and water. The cruel restrictions soon led to starvation and disease, causing hundreds of people to perish.

During the day when her parents were at work, Rózia stayed with Szymek's wife, Paula, and two-year-old son, Moshe. Occasionally, the little girl would venture outside. But after witnessing several sidewalk executions—including one when SS men, laughing, shot a pregnant woman for the fun of it—Rózia would dash into the nearest apartment building or cellar the moment she saw any SS officer or German soldier.

The Nazis heightened the terror by murdering 35 Jews in the ghetto on April 30 and then, two weeks later, marched another 250 into a nearby forest and machine-gunned them.

In June, thousands of Jews from surrounding towns and villages were transported to Rzeszow, swelling the combined population of the two ghettos to 23,000.

A few weeks later, all the ghetto residents were forced to assemble at the *Sammelplatz*, where the Nazis split up families, pulling out the elderly and the sick. When people protested, soldiers fired into the crowd and let snarling guard dogs loose to attack them. Toward the back of the petrified mob, Rózia couldn't see the mayhem, but she could hear screams, shouts, barking, and gunfire. Trembling with dread, she crouched between her mother and father, wishing she could be invisible, wishing she could be back home.

Police rounded up about 2,000 elderly and sick Jews, trucked them to the forest, and shot them. Then another 4,000 were herded to the train station. Along the way, they were clubbed and beaten, and more than 40 were shot. Packed into cattle cars and taken away, they were never heard from again.

Days later, the Nazis posted a list of mothers and children of workers of the smaller ghetto who had to report to the *Sammelplatz*. They were told they would be transported to a work camp that had day care and school for the kids. Among those on the list was Uncle Szymek's wife, Paula, and son, Moshe.

Sabina, who was required to continue her culvert-laying job, thought the work camp would be an excellent opportunity for Rózia to leave the ghetto. Holding Rózia by the hand, Sabina went to Paula and said, "When you're gone, I'll have no one to care for Rózia during the day. Please take her with you."

Rózia gazed at her aunt with pleading eyes, hoping Paula would say yes.

"I'm sorry, Sabina, but I can't take her," Paula replied. "I'll hold my son by one hand and my purse in the other."

Disappointment and sadness enveloped Rózia because she would be spending her days alone in the apartment and have nobody to play with.

Later that day, August 7, about 1,000 women and children were loaded into cattle cars. When Szymek returned home from work and heard that his wife and son were on the transport, he raced to the railroad station, arriving just as the train was pulling out. He and other husbands whose wives and children were on the transport chased after it. Some of the men succeeded in climbing onboard. Szymek was among the many who couldn't catch up to the train. Later that evening, a broken-hearted Szymek and others gathered in grief and wept over their loved ones, whose fate, at the moment, was unknown.

They soon found out. A family friend whose wife, children, and mother had been taken away had a key to a Nazi warehouse in town. He learned that the train had gone to Belzec, a city in southeastern Poland that had an extermination camp. The train had returned to Rzeszow with piles of used clothes that were unloaded into the warehouse. The friend was sorting clothes when he recognized his mother's coat and children's shoes.

It was later discovered that at the Belzec death camp, Jews were gassed on arrival. Throughout the month, another 18,000 Jews from Rzeszow were sent to their deaths—a horrific loss that was kept hidden from the 4,000 remaining Jews.

Toward the end of August, the Nazis announced another *Aktion*, requiring certain residents of the smaller ghetto to report to the *Sammelplatz* in two days. Many feared it meant all nonessential workers and the remaining children would be taken to Belzec for extermination.

Before dawn the next morning, Sabina helped Ròzia get dressed and told her, "You're coming with me." At the ghetto entrance, the two walked up to a guard, a Polish policeman whom Sabina knew. "I need to take my daughter with me to work because I have nowhere to leave her," Sabina told him.

He let them pass. It was dawn when Sabina and Ròzia joined the group of workers heading out to their jobs on the roads and culverts. As soon as they crossed into the Aryan side, Sabina let go of Ròzia's hand, pointed to a middle-aged woman standing across the street, and said, "Don't run, just walk slowly over to that lady."

Never questioning her mother, Ròzia obediently strolled to the stranger. The woman took the child's hand and led her to an apartment a few blocks away. Once inside, the woman closed all the windows and lowered the shades. She told Ròzia, "Stay in the bedroom and don't make a sound. I have to go to work." She left, locking the door behind her.

Having no time to mentally and emotionally prepare for this abrupt change in her life, the frightened seven-year-old girl broke down and wept. Her mother had never said a word about this, had never even said good-bye or given her a kiss. Ròzia was in a stranger's apartment with no idea why or for how long. It was too much for her. She cried all day. When the woman returned that evening, Ròzia was still sobbing. She pleaded, "I want to go home. I want to see my mother and father."

"All right," said the woman. First, though, she cut open the hem of the girl's green coat and took out all the money that Sabina had sewn inside it. The money was meant to pay for Ròzia's care for several weeks. Later that night, the woman escorted Ròzia to a barbed-wire fence bordering the ghetto and pushed her through an opening at the bottom.

Ròzia ran straight home, threw open the bedroom door, saw her father in bed, and squealed, "*Tatus!*" (Polish for "Papa.")

Jozef broke out in a huge grin. Calling her by a pet Yiddish name meaning Little Rose, he held out his hands and exclaimed, "Reisele! You're back!" Without taking off her coat, Ròzia leaped into his arms. They held each other tightly, barely saying another word. They didn't have to talk. They were just so happy to be together again. Rózia fell fast asleep in his arms, still in her clothes.

Around midnight, Sabina, tired from another long day at her two jobs, returned to the apartment. Rózia sat up in bed and smiled, thinking her mother would be thrilled to see her. But Sabina's reaction was just the opposite. Flinging her hands to her head, Sabina gasped in shock, her face turning white in panic. There would be no hugs or kisses.

Seeing her mother's expression of alarm, Rózia's happiness vanished instantly. *I did something wrong,* she thought. *I should've stayed with that woman.*

Sabina didn't scold Rózia. Instead, she turned to her husband and said, "All mothers and children must show up at the *Sammelplatz* in the morning. She can't be there. I must look for a place for her to hide."

Sabina didn't get any sleep. Throughout the night, she scoured the apartment building from the basement to the rooftop, searching for a hiding place for Rózia. Nothing was suitable. She had one other option: Before dawn, she talked to the friendly guard at the ghetto entrance. In a stroke of luck, he wasn't aware of the *Aktion* that was supposed to occur later that morning at the *Sammelplatz,* so he agreed to let Sabina bring Rózia to work. Sabina knew that if the Nazis found out, the two of them would likely be executed on the spot.

About 5:00 a.m., mother and daughter went through the checkpoint. As they walked with the workers toward their jobs, Sabina took Rόzia's hand and, when the guards weren't looking, led her out of the line. They scurried off in the darkness to a nearby Catholic cemetery, where they hid behind two large tombstones.

A few minutes later, they heard shouts and gunfire coming from the ghetto entrance. Other Jews were also trying to escape rather than face the *Aktion*. At morning light, Sabina whispered to Rόzia, "We can't stay here any longer or they'll find us."

She knew someone she hoped would help them—Ludwig Richter,* her civilian supervisor at work. Richter was a kind and gentle *Volksdeutsche*, who was increasingly distressed over the mistreatment of Jews. He had told Sabina, "If you ever need help, come see me."

Sabina and Rόzia dashed to his apartment, which was across the street from the cemetery, and woke him up. After Sabina explained their dilemma, Richter said, "Let me see what I can do. You both look very tired. While I'm gone, why don't you two lie down and get some rest." They both fell asleep within minutes.

Soon, Richter returned with a fake Polish passport for Sabina and arranged for someone to look after Rόzia while Sabina sneaked back into the larger ghetto to say goodbye to her sisters Rozia and Balbina.

When Sabina told them about the escape, her sister Rozia begged, "Take my little girl with you. Save Belusia."

"How can I?" Sabina responded. "I don't even know if I can save Rózia and myself." As much as it pained her, Sabina left without Belusia.

With her heart breaking because there was a good chance she would never see her beloved sisters or niece again, Sabina went to meet Jozef one last time. He couldn't go with her because he had no papers that would allow him to leave the ghetto. As they embraced, he said, "Save yourself and our daughter."

Sabina collected some precious family photos for safe-keeping and left. The next day, she and Rózia headed to Warsaw on the train. During the trip, Sabina had second thoughts about the photos because so many were of relatives who looked Jewish. Afraid that if the photos were found on her, they would give her away as a Jew, she tore them up and flushed them down the toilet.

In January 1943, shortly after Rózia turned eight, Sabina and another woman interviewed for a job as a live-in house-keeper for Adam Zak, a widowed gentile banker who lived near the Warsaw Ghetto. He had a 14-year-old daughter, Hanka, and a 21-year-old son, Marian.

After Zak questioned the women in front of Hanka, he asked his daughter, "Which one would you like to be our housekeeper?" When Hanka pointed to Sabina, he took the girl aside and whispered, "She's Jewish. Are you sure you want her? She also has a young daughter."

"I don't care that she's Jewish," Hanka said. "I want her."

Sabina was hired. The other woman was furious, but she didn't pose a problem because Marian ended up marrying her. Eventually, she worked for the Polish underground with Marian until the Nazis captured him and sent him to Auschwitz, where he was murdered.

For Rózia, life became a series of living—or, more accurately, hiding—in strangers' homes. An apartment in Warsaw, a house in Radom, a farm outside Ostroleka. A few weeks here, a few weeks there. The length of time depended on how long it took for neighbors to become suspicious before she was uprooted and shipped off to the next place. The little girl sometimes didn't see her mother for weeks at a time, and when she did, it was only for a few hours.

Rózia had a new identity—Halinka. But no matter what she called herself, she felt like an orphan. Her father, she assumed, was still trapped in the ghetto and her mother was always gone. Adding to her emotional turmoil, at whatever home was sheltering her, Rózia was supposed to call her mother Pani Zak (Mrs. Zak) or sometimes Ciocia (Auntie), but never Mother. Her cover story was that her mom was a non-Jew who worked in Warsaw, and her dad was a soldier fighting for the Germans. Sabina was either a family friend or aunt who worked long hours in Warsaw and was trying to find a permanent home for the girl.

Rózia never questioned why the secrecy, why the pretending, why she had to hide though her mother didn't. She just accepted it as a way of life, as a way to avoid the grip of that evil man, Adolf Hitler, who, she was convinced, personally wanted to kill her.

Whenever Sabina couldn't find a home for Rózia, the girl temporarily stayed with her at the Zak residence. Rózia loved those moments because she could be with her mother and also spend time with Hanka, who treated her warmly as a little sister. Hanka played with her and combed her hair, even when it was infested with lice.

No one other than the Zak family was supposed to know that Rózia was in the apartment. The doorbell was Rózia's signal to hide in a bedroom armoire and curl up with a pillow until guests left, which was often late into the night. In the dark armoire, Rózia replayed in her mind memories of sitting in her father's lap, listening to him sing to her as he worked on a new pair of shoes. She always expected him to show up and whisk her away to a safe haven. The daydream never died.

In summer 1943, Rózia went to live with the Nowaks*, a caring, childless, Catholic couple who had a Warsaw apartment above the stationery store they owned. She overheard her mother tell Mrs. Nowak, "If worse comes to worst, and something bad happens to me, you can convert my daughter to Catholicism."

The Nowaks were kind to Rózia and took her to church with them so she could learn about their religion. They were teaching her the rosary and preparing her to receive the sacrament of Holy Communion. In July, shortly before the big day, Rozia was sitting in front of the mirror, fixing her hair and humming a tune. She was happy because she was going to get a white dress to wear to communion. *I won't have to be afraid anymore,* she thought. *I'll be like everyone else and play with the children outside and have fun.* Becoming a Catholic didn't bother her. She knew little of Jewish doctrine because she hadn't been taught much about the faith of her parents, who weren't Orthodox Jews and didn't keep a kosher home.

Just days before the scheduled communion, Rozia was tending the store while the Nowaks were having lunch. Unexpectedly, authorities arrived. They had been tipped off that a Jew lived above the store. Seeing Mr. Nowak's dark wavy hair and brown eyes, they assumed he was the Jew the tipster was talking about and arrested him. The Nazis checked him out, confirmed he was a gentile, and released him. By then, a stranger had come for Rozia and taken her to another place to hide. Leaving the Nowaks was a crushing disappointment to the girl because she had felt so comfortable with them.

Fear, loneliness, and sadness shadowed Rozia at every residence she stayed, no matter how nice the family was. She looked forward to her mother's infrequent visits. During one such visit, Sabina tucked her into bed, kneeled beside her, and stroked her hair. It was the closest Rozia had ever felt to her mother. Sabina then whispered a simple Yiddish prayer and said, "Don't forget to say this every night. It will help make things better."

The prayer, which rhymed in Yiddish, loosely translated to

"In God's name, I lay me down with all my limbs. May I wake up tomorrow again, healthy and whole. In God's name, amen." Rôzia recited the prayer every night, believing it would save her life and keep her close to her mother. It gave her hope.

At one apartment, she stayed with a gentile couple who had a little boy she played with during the day while the parents were at work. The drapes were always kept closed, and Rôzia had strict instructions to remain inside. "Do not look out the window," the mother told her. "Children play in the courtyard, and if they spot you and you don't go out and play, they will suspect you are Jewish."

But, being a curious eight-year-old, Rôzia simply couldn't resist when she heard kids laughing outside. She opened the drapes, lifted the shade, and peeked down at the children. At that moment, a boy looked up. When Rôzia realized he saw her, she ducked behind the shade.

The next day, an unsigned letter was slipped under the front door. It said, "If you don't send the Jew away, we will give her away."

Once again, Rôzia was abruptly moved to another place. She figured the neighbor boy who spotted her had told his parents, and they were the ones who wrote the note. *At least they sent a letter and didn't go straight to the police*, she thought.

Rôzia was in constant fear of the Germans, and she was grateful to the people who risked their own lives to harbor her. They certainly weren't doing it for the money that Sabina gave them, which was barely enough to cover the cost of the girl's food.

Eventually, it became too difficult for Sabina to find a safe place for Rózia. Having the girl hide for any length of time at Mr. Zak's apartment was out of the question. Then Mr. Zak came up with a drastic solution: He pulled Hanka, who was then 16, out of school and sent her and Rózia to live with a distant relative on a farm outside of Warsaw. Hanka pretended to be Rózia's big sister and acted as her protector. Mr. Zak told Hanka that by having her go with Rózia, there was less of a chance that neighbors there would be suspicious. However, he told her, "If you encounter any trouble, you find the nearest phone and call me immediately."

The new family wasn't particularly friendly toward Rózia. They made her eat out of the cat's dish and gave her the worst errands. Once, she had to stand in line at the village store for milk in the dead of winter for several hours even though she had no gloves and wore a coat that was way too small for her. Seeing how miserable the girl was, Hanka felt sorry for her and took her place in line.

In many ways, Hanka suffered as much as Rózia. The family was poor and didn't have a lot of food to share, so she often went hungry. She missed school, learning, sleeping in her own bed, and gossiping with her girlfriends. She missed her dad. But this was where she needed to be—with Rózia—because the teenager felt responsible for the girl's safety.

By age nine, Rózia had gained some street smarts. She knew not to act intimidated if she encountered anyone who accused her of being Jewish. One day she was carrying home a watermelon when several bullies circled her and called her a little Jew and other names. *If I run, I'll be giving myself away*, she thought. It wasn't easy, but she remained stone-faced and walked at a regular pace back to the farmhouse.

Another time, Rózia was in the village when a Nazi officer walked toward her. *Don't look away or look down*, she told herself. *If I do, he'll think I'm scared of him because I'm Jewish.* The truth was, she *was* scared of him, so much so that she had trouble breathing. But as they passed each other, she had enough gumption to look him straight in the eye and nod. She didn't start breathing normally again until she reached the corner.

Rózia always worried that some bad person would discover she was a Jew. One night, she and Hanka were sleeping in the bed they shared at the farmhouse when the Gestapo banged on the front door. Hearing scuffling and shouting in the other room, Hanka whispered, "They're coming for you!"

Rózia was seized with terror. So she did what most kids in this kind of a frightening situation would do—she hid under the covers.

Fortunately for the girl, the Gestapo didn't want her. They came for the oldest son in the family. Accusing him of working for the Polish underground, they hauled him away.

The relief Rózia felt didn't last long. Just days later, the family received one of those unsigned notes that she knew so well: "You are keeping a Jew. Send her away immediately or we will expose her."

After reading the note, Rózia and Hanka hurriedly packed their things and ran away. Taking off their shoes, they raced for several miles until they found a phone they could use. Hanka called her father, who picked them up and brought them back to Warsaw.

While Rózia was hiding out temporarily in the Zak apartment, Sabina was troubled about where to place her next. One day, they heard police sirens. The building custodian, who never gave an inkling that he knew Sabina and Rózia were Jewish, saw them in the hallway and warned, "The gendarmes are coming!"

The sirens grew louder. Sabina took Rózia's hand and scampered up to the top of the five-story building and onto the flat roof. Rózia was bewildered as she went with her mother to the edge. The police cars were closer now.

The girl knew to be afraid because authorities were always after Jews. But she didn't know why she and her mother were standing so close to the roof's edge. And she certainly didn't know that her mother was thinking, *If they come for us, we will protect the Zak family. We will jump to our deaths together.*

The police cars pulled even with the front of the building and then stopped a few doors down. For several tense minutes, mother and daughter stood silently, still holding hands. Suddenly, the door to the roof opened. It was the custodian. "It's okay to come down," he told them. Rózia and Sabina were safe—at least for another day.

In August 1944, a large group of Polish resisters known as the Home Army tried to wrest control of Warsaw from the Germans in what became known as the Warsaw Uprising. After 63 days of fierce fighting, the Germans prevailed and then set out to destroy the entire city.

Sabina, Rózia, and Hanka fled Warsaw during the uprising and wandered from village to village for four grueling months. The girls were reduced to knocking on the doors of peasants and begging for food. Somehow, they found an unoccupied farmhouse and stayed there while Sabina went back to Warsaw, although she visited them often.

In December 1944, Rózia and Hanka were in the house when they were caught in the middle of a deadly battle between retreating German forces and the advancing Red Army. Artillery shells shrieked overhead and bullets flew in all directions. Blasts from cannon fire and mortar rounds shook the house. For protection, the helpless girls hunkered down behind an old piano.

After hours of intense, deafening fighting, all became silent. The girls remained huddled, wondering who had won this skirmish. Then they heard footsteps approaching the house. *Are they Germans or Russians?* Rózia wondered. She figured if they were Germans, her life was over. The door swung open and in came Russian soldiers, holding harmonicas and bottles of vodka. The troops smiled at the startled girls and then began singing and drinking in victory.

"We've been liberated," Hanka said.

As the reality of this glorious news sank in, Rózia's whole body began to relax. It was a wonderful sensation she hadn't felt since the last time she was tucked into her bed with the blue satin sheets trimmed in lace. What made the feeling even better was a simple but powerful thought that popped into her head: *I don't have to be afraid of the Germans anymore.*

Much of Warsaw had been leveled by the Germans. Mr. Zak's apartment building had been destroyed, although he was safe. He found a different place to live and went back to work at the bank.

In early 1945, Sabina and Rózia, who was now 10, returned to Kalisz, hoping to reunite with loved ones. Hanka came with them. When they entered the apartment, they discovered it had been looted. But neighbors in the building told Sabina the names of those who took her furniture, and she was able to get most everything back.

Rózia's father did not survive the Holocaust. Although no one knows exactly how Jozef was murdered, it's thought that when the Rzeszow ghetto was liquidated, he was among the last taken to a nearby cemetery and executed.

Szymek was spared and survived several concentration camps. His wife, Paula, and son, Moshe, were gassed upon arrival at

Belzec. So, too, were Ròzia's aunts Balbina and Rozia and cousin Belusia. The only other member of Ròzia's extended family who survived was a cousin.

Even though the war was over, life didn't get much better for Polish Jews because they were harassed by anti-Semitic Poles. After 42 Jewish Holocaust survivors in Kielce, Poland, were murdered, Sabina decided she and Ròzia would leave the country. She asked Hanka, who was like a daughter to her, to join them. But Hanka chose to remain near her father, so Sabina gave her the apartment and furnishings.

After spending a few months at a displaced persons camp in Germany, mother and daughter settled in Munich, where Ròzia went to Hebrew school and Sabina remarried. In 1951, when Ròzia was 16, the family emigrated to the United States and settled in Cleveland, Ohio. Szymek came with them.

Sabina suffered from depression and died of a heart attack in 1970 at age 65. Szymek, who Americanized his name to Simon, worked in a factory as a toolmaker. He also battled depression and had several strokes. He died in 1996 at age 94.

Ròzia, now called Rose, married Holocaust survivor Arthur Gelbart in 1955, and together they raised two children while running a flooring company. Rose is the president of Child Survivors of the Holocaust and Descendants in Northeast Ohio, which she established in 1994. She also is active in the World Federation of Jewish Child Survivors of the Holocaust.

"I carried a lot of emotional baggage," recalls Rose. "After liberation, we kids were happy to be children again, but nobody ever talked to us about what we went through. The teachers figured if we don't talk about it, we will forget. But you don't forget. It's ingrained. It even gets worse. The trauma of a lost childhood can never be recaptured. I missed hugs because no one ever hugged me. Everyone lived in fear. Mother would never talk about my father or what I had gone through. It was like the Holocaust never happened to us."

Rose, now the grandmother of four, has made six trips to Poland and visited with Hanka several times, but the two didn't spend much time talking about those horrible days. Hanka, who never finished school, married, had two children, divorced, and remarried. "Hanka showed unbelievable courage for a teenager," says Rose. "She could have had a normal childhood during the German occupation in Warsaw, but she chose instead to hide with me and protect me as my sister despite the danger. She lived in fear with me. She knew her fate would be the same as mine had we been caught. During the war, she never once mentioned to anyone—even her closest relatives—that my mother and I were Jewish. She kept it a secret." Rózia said Hanka, whose last name is Janczak, lives in a nursing home.

In 1995, Adam Zak and Hanka were recognized by Yad Vashem as Righteous Among the Nations.

GLOSSARY

Aktion German word for the roundup, deportation, or murder of Jews

Allies countries such as the United States, Great Britain, and the Soviet Union that fought against Nazi Germany, Italy, and Japan during World War II

Anschluss German annexation of Austria in March 1938

anti-Semitic referring to the opposition to or discrimination of Jews

anti-Semitism dislike or hatred of Jews

Appell lengthy roll call of prisoners, who often were forced to stand outside in all types of weather

Aryan term used by Nazis to describe "racially superior" northern European physical characteristics such as blond hair and blue eyes

Axis powers Nazi Germany, Italy, and Japan and several smaller Eastern European and Slavic countries during World War II

babushka woman's head scarf, folded in a triangle and worn tied under the chin

crematorium oven built in a concentration camp to burn and dispose of the bodies of murdered people

deportation the removing of Jews from their homes or ghettoes to concentration camps

DP displaced person, one of millions of survivors, soldiers, and civilians who either couldn't or wouldn't return to their former homes in Europe after the war

extermination camp one of six major death camps in Nazi-occupied Poland built solely to kill Jews—Auschwitz-Birkenau, Belzec, Chelmno, Majdanek, Sobibor, and Treblinka

Führer German word for "leader" adopted by Adolf Hitler as his title

gendarme during the Holocaust, this French word for "policeman" took on the special meaning of a pro-Nazi armed police officer or a soldier serving as a policeman

gentile person who is not Jewish

Gestapo short for German name for Secret State Police of the Nazi German army, organized to stamp out any political opposition

ghetto small section of a city where Jews were forced to live, separated from the rest of the city by walls and barbed wire fences

Jehovah's Witnesses members of a Christian sect who were persecuted by the Nazis for refusal to swear allegiance to Hitler and the Nazis

Judenfrei German expression meaning "cleansed of all Jews"

Judenrat council of Jewish leaders handpicked by authorities to carry out Nazi orders in the ghetto or occupied area

Kapo prisoner, usually Jewish, who had special privileges and cooperated with the Nazis in concentration camps, often intimidating and punishing fellow inmates

kibbutz communal settlement in Israel, typically a farm

liberation the freeing of someone from imprisonment, oppression, or occupation

liquidation removal or elimination of people through murder; the destruction or termination of a ghetto, camp, or village

Molotov cocktail crude fire-starting bomb typically consisting of a bottle filled with flammable liquid

Nazi name for a member of the National Socialist Democratic Workers Party who believed in Aryan supremacy

partisan organized guerilla fighter who attacked German military targets, often using the forest for cover

pogrom organized, and often officially encouraged, massacre or attack on Jews

Red Army military forces of the Soviet Union

resettlement German code word for the deportation of prisoners to death camps

SA *Sturmabteilung* also known as Brownshirts or storm troopers, the terrorist branch of the Nazi army, which was used to help secure Hitler's rise to power

Selektion German term describing the process of separating Jewish victims for either slave labor or death

Sonderkommandos work units of Jewish prisoners forced to haul dead bodies out of gas chambers and toss them into crematoriums to burn

SS *Schutzstaffel* the German army's elite guard organized to serve as Hitler's personal protectors and to administer concentration camps

Star of David six-pointed star, which is a symbol of Judaism

swastika ancient symbol, once used to ward off evil spirits, adopted by the Nazis as their official insignia

Torah first five books of the Hebrew Bible

transport train of overcrowded boxcars crammed with mostly Jewish victims bound for concentration camps

typhus infectious disease carried by lice or fleas, which resulted in many deaths in concentration camps and ghettos

underground organized group acting in secrecy to resist occupying enemy forces

Volksdeutsche German Aryan who lives in a country other than Germany

Waffen-SS militarized units of the SS

Wehrmacht regular German armed forces

Yad Vashem Israel's official Holocaust memorial, located in Jerusalem, which consists of the Holocaust History Museum, Children's Memorial, Hall of Remembrance, and the Museum of Holocaust Art; it is a research institute with archives and a library, among other facilities; also, on behalf of the State of Israel and the Jewish people, Yad Vashem awards the title of Righteous Among the Nations to gentiles who risked their lives to save Jews during the Holocaust

Yiddish a language, mostly based on a combination of Hebrew and German, spoken by many Jews in Eastern Europe

ABOUT THE AUTHOR

Allan Zullo is the author of more than 100 nonfiction books on subjects ranging from sports and the supernatural to history and animals.

He has introduced Scholastic readers to the Ten True Tales series, gripping stories of extraordinary persons who have met the challenges of dangerous, sometimes life-threatening situations. Among the books in the series are *Heroes of Pearl Harbor*; *Vietnam War Heroes*; *World War I Heroes*; *World War II Heroes*; *War Heroes: Voices from Iraq*; *Battle Heroes: Voices from Afghanistan*; *Young Civil Rights Heroes*; and *Heroes of 9/11*. In addition, he has authored four books about the real-life experiences of young people during the Holocaust—*Survivors: True Stories of Children in the Holocaust*; *Heroes of the Holocaust: True Stories of Rescues by Teens*; *Escape: Children of the Holocaust*; and *We Fought Back: Teen Resisters of the Holocaust*.

Allan, the father of two grown daughters and the grandfather of five, lives with his wife, Kathryn, near Asheville, North Carolina. To learn more about the author, visit his website at www.allanzullo.com.